YOUTH SUNDAY
Every SUNDAY

A Series Of Sermons Devoted To Youth

Dr. Terry Thomas

Author of "Making It Through A Storm"

Edited by
Benjamin Thomas, Jr.

Reviewed by
The Wife and The Siblings of Rev. Dr. Terry Thomas

authorHOUSE®

AuthorHouse™
1663 Liberty Drive
Bloomington, IN 47403
www.authorhouse.com
Phone: 833-262-8899

Published by AuthorHouse 11/27/2020

ISBN: 978-1-6655-0609-0 (sc)
ISBN: 978-1-6655-0607-6 (hc)
ISBN: 978-1-6655-0608-3 (e)

Library of Congress Control Number: 2020921376

Print information available on the last page.

Contents

Acknowledgments...vii
Foreword..ix
Introduction...xi

Chapter 1   The Story of the Cracker Jack: Doing Just a
Little Bit More 1
Chapter 2   Learning to Shine Wherever You Are 13
Chapter 3   Slumbering and Sleeping at the Wrong Time 24
Chapter 4   A Lesson from Balaam: Learning to Listen
to Those Who See What You Do Not See....................35
Chapter 5   David's Armament against Goliath: A
Good Sense of Self-Worth 46
Chapter 6   The Key to Succeeding: Believing in Yourself............. 57
Chapter 7   Learning to Move Beyond an Encounter
with Disappointment 68
Chapter 8   What to Do When Seemingly Successful
Steps Lead to Disappointments? 83
Chapter 9   Sticking with It until You Get It.................................. 95
Chapter 10 From Comfortable Strength to Frightened
Helplessness by a Great Loss..107
Chapter 11 The Demise of Letting Our Guards Down 117
Chapter 12 Beware of Satan Disguised as a Friend 128
Chapter 13 Making the Most of a Rare Opportunity....................138
Chapter 14 Synchronizing Purpose and Time 147
Chapter 15 Developing My Innate Blessing: Learning
Self-Reliance 155
Chapter 16 Helping Our Children to Walk on Water....................166
Chapter 17 A Response to a Baby's Cry: Compassion....................177

End Notes...189
The Author 193

ACKNOWLEDGMENTS

A TRIBUTE TO THE LIFE OF REV. DR. TERRY THOMAS
(November 13, 1959 – April 23, 2016)

God gave the Late Rev. Dr. Terry Thomas a strong passion for writing which led him to author five books before his death on April 23, 2016. Prior to his death, he had just released *"Divine Inspiration for Victorious Living"* on April 18, 2016. In addition, he was preparing the manuscript for this book which he titled *"Youth Sunday Every Sunday"*. He was terribly excited about this book. He had planned it to be a compilation of sermons dedicated to giving spiritual guidance and encouragement to young people and to parents. By the grace of God, this book is being published as a memorial to his life and legacy. His 30 years of laboring in the Word of God were blessed beyond measure. God worked through him until He determined the time had come to give him eternal rest from all his labor. His memories and his works remain forever dear and precious to his family and to all who came to know him as a Faithful Servant of God.

In his honor, recognition is given to his wife and his twelve siblings for coming together to review and to publish this book. Special gratitude to Valerie Thomas (his wife). Special thanks to his sisters (Teresa Jackson, Patricia Goodwin, Vickie Furman, Gail Thomas, Cathy Hall, Annette Thomas, Sandra Faye Walton, Chenequia Simpson, and Tonnia Thomas). Special appreciation to his brothers (Benjamin Thomas Jr, Daryl Thomas, and Tony Thomas). We also recognize two of his sisters-in-laws who supported the review and publishing of this book (Betty Thomas and Carolyne Thomas). May the wisdom God gave to our beloved Rev. Dr. Terry Thomas bless the lives of many young people, including all his nieces and nephews.

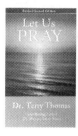

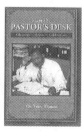

FOREWORD

The sermons of this book were written, preached, selected, compiled, and ordered by the Late Rev. Dr. Terry Thomas. They were to be the first volume for this book which bears the title *Youth Sunday Every Sunday*.

Prior to his death, Dr. Thomas had planned to compile 52 sermons dedicated to youth. These would be sermons he had prepared during the 30 years of his pastoral ministry. During these years, he religiously dedicated himself to preparing a sermon per month devoted to youth.

In planning for this book, Dr. Thomas wanted to emphasize the need to preach and teach spiritual and practical life lessons to help youth develop sound Christian character that would help them mature spiritually and morally. Through this book, his desire was to help youth develop values they would need to build a strong foundation for their lives.

After compiling this initial set of sermons and forwarding them to his elder brother on April 21, 2016, Dr. Thomas went home to be with the Lord very suddenly on April 23, 2016. We are hereby compelled to carry-forward the work Dr. Thomas left with us. We are delighted to present this book as the last work of his ministry while he was present on earth.

The sermons herein were edited for publication by his elder brother but the substance and the content of each are completely the works of Dr. Terry Thomas. The sermons compiled here reflect his labor in the Word of God and his ability to see reflections of God's Word in all areas of life. Thus, his sermons are full of good practical wisdom derived from his spiritual insights from the Word of God. Clearly, God gave him to glean an understanding of truth from many personalities around the world, from his own personal experiences, and from diverse situations of life that impact youth.

As the Lord grants grace, perhaps there will be additional volumes of this book to emerge from Dr. Thomas's treasures of sermons devoted to youth which he preached during his pastorate of three churches: First Baptist Church (New Hill, NC); Mount Zion Baptist Church (Madison, WI); and West Durham Baptist Church (Durham, NC). May God continue to bless his love for truth; and may God bless the legacy of his ministry to give light and liberty to all who have heard him proclaim the Word of God and to all who read his works.

By Benjamin Thomas, Jr. (Eldest Brother of Rev. Dr. Terry Thomas)

INTRODUCTION

One of the important lessons of life is that our lives tend to change with time, and each context of life is not necessarily the same. Right now, I am going through what I want to refer to as a time adjustment. Some of the many things that I have become extremely comfortable with are no longer being widely used. Subsequently, to some degree, I feel out of touch with time.

This may not be the case for some today; or for others who grew up in larger settings than the one I experienced. Nevertheless, I was reared in a church located in a small rural southern town. It was not my experience to hear sermons often directed toward the youth. To be honest, I hardly ever heard a sermon directed toward the youth except for the annual Youth Day. After moving from the rural south and living in midsize urban cities, I found my expeience to be basically the same. For reasons which I cannot fully explain, a devotion to preparing sermons that directly address and focus on the life and situations of the youth does not appear to be embraced.

Since 1986, I have been blessed with the privilege to serve as pastor of a church. The first church to which that privilege was bestowed upon me was the First Baptist Church, New Hill, North Carolina. Beginning with my first month as pastor of the First Baptist Church, I made the commitment to always preach a youth sermon at least once of month. Upon becoming pastor of the Mount Zion Baptist Church, Madison, Wisconsin, and the West Durham Baptist Church, Durham, North Carolina, I held to that commitment.

It fascinates me the way time moves! It is kind of hard to believe that I started writing youth sermons once a month 30 years ago (since 1986). When I started writing sermons devoted to youth, I would have never predicted 30 years later that I would be led to look through those hundreds of youth sermons and select some to comprise a book entitled *Youth Sunday Every Sunday*. I must confess, at the start 30 years ago, it was unbeknown to me that I had begun seeking those values that would help the youth build strong foundations for their lives.

I am quite sure that there are many churches across the land with what many call "children's church". There are also churches which have the benefit of having a youth pastor to provide messages for their youth. On the other hand, some churches may not be as fortunate. This book, *Youth Sunday Every Sunday*, is intended to be a four-volume series designed to help churches have a message for the youth each Sunday in a year. Ultimately, the main intent of this book is to assist the youth in establishing strong foundations upon which to build their lives. A more philosophical expression of that would be to help the youth develop spiritual guidance and wisdom. The idea is to help our youth develop godly wisdom that will guide them in making good decisions and in living an abundantly fruitful life.

When I graduated from Tuskegee University in 1982 with a Bachelor of Science in Mathematics/Computer Science, I was given a job with IBM in Raleigh, North Carolina. Before leaving for the job, I made the following statement one Sunday morning during Sunday School at my home church (St. Paul A.M.E. Church, Hurtsboro, Alabama): *"I have acquired skills to make a living, but now I also need to gain skills to teach me how to live."* In my pursuit of trying to obtain a good life, I have since learned that the most important things we need to have an abundantly fruitful and productive life are not often given much attention. Often, we make the mistake of gaining and obtaining things without knowing how to make the most of what we have in our possession. Life can become very difficult without any guidance on how to live and can perhaps be the source of much unhappiness.

The objective of *Youth Sunday Every Sunday* is to offer a collection of inspirational messages (or sermons, if you like) to address many fundamental values which are essential for a good life. It is my prayer and hope that these messages will be a tremendous blessing in helping prepare our youth for a very vigorous and productive life. Therefore, I release to you the first *Youth Sunday Every Sunday*.

1

The Story of the Cracker Jack: Doing Just a Little Bit More

Competition is just a normal human interaction. There is often just one position to be fulfilled, but many competing for that one position. With many people competing for a single position, what is it that can cause one to positively standout from others competing for that one position? In this sermon, Dr. Thomas illustrates how doing a little bit more than what is required or expected can have a great impact on one being selected among others for a particular task or position. Therefore, the objective of this sermon is to stress to youth the great value of doing just a little bit more than what is required or asked of you.

Text: Genesis 24:15-26 (KJV)

[15] And it came to pass, before he had done speaking, that, behold, Rebekah came out, who was born to Bethuel, son of Milcah, the wife of Nahor, Abraham's brother, with her pitcher upon her shoulder.

[16] And the damsel *was* very fair to look upon, a virgin, neither had any man known her: and she went down to the well, and filled her pitcher, and came up.

[17] And the servant ran to meet her, and said, Let me, I pray thee, drink a little water of thy pitcher.

[18] And she said, Drink, my lord: and she hasted, and let down her pitcher upon her hand, and gave him drink.

[19] And when she had done giving him drink, she said, I will draw *water* for thy camels also, until they have done drinking.

²⁰ And she hasted, and emptied her pitcher into the trough, and ran again unto the well to draw *water*, and drew for all his camels.

²¹ And the man wondering at her held his peace, to wit whether the LORD had made his journey prosperous or not.

²² And it came to pass, as the camels had done drinking, that the man took a golden earring of half a shekel weight, and two bracelets for her hands of ten *shekels* weight of gold:

²³ And said, Whose daughter *art* thou? tell me, I pray thee: is there room *in* thy father's house for us to lodge in?

²⁴ And she said unto him, I *am* the daughter of Bethuel the son of Milcah, which she bare unto Nahor.

²⁵ She said moreover unto him, We have both straw and provender enough, and room to lodge in.

²⁶ And the man bowed down his head, and worshiped the LORD.

It might be hard for some to believe, but there are perhaps a few people who grew up in the 60s, 70s, and 80s who do not know about Cracker Jacks. This certainly excludes me as a by-product of an extremely small rural town in Alabama. Some of my most thrilling times as a little boy were having a box of Cracker Jacks. Though that was many years ago, my interest in Cracker Jacks resurfaced after I came across a story about Cracker Jacks in a book by Don Gabor entitled, *Big Things Happen When You Do the Little Things Right*.

Don Gabor's story about Cracker Jacks opened my eyes to the secret behind those who are given special recognition or presented the privilege to experience certain opportunities in life. The secret, by no stretch of the imagination, was not complex. Rather it was simple. The secret was *a willingness just to do a little bit more*. In case you are wondering, let me share with you what I read in Don Gabor's book that brought that insight to me. Gabor wrote:

> *Nearly everyone living in America has munched on Cracker Jacks, the candy-coated popcorn and peanut snack, but did you ever wonder how it got to be so popular? It wasn't the only product of this kind on the market - in fact, far from it. By the early 1900s, there were more than one hundred brands of similar-tasting candy, including Yellow Kid, Honey Corn, Little Buster, and Razzle Dazzle, to name just a few. Yet, after nearly a hundred years, only Cracker Jacks still satisfies millions sweet tooths around the country, while the other brands have long disappeared. Why?*
>
> *[Well], Cracker Jacks won the hearts of snack-food lovers because its inventor came up with an innovative marketing idea: he included a small prize in each box. The success story of the Cracker Jacks, like so many other success stories, hinged on a stroke of creativity that set this product apart from its competition.[1]*

From that reading, you can perhaps tell what became the success of the Cracker Jacks. Although there were more than a hundred similar brands, it was the owner's willingness to *do just a little bit more* that brought him success. He did not change the taste of candy-coated popcorn. He did what all the other brands of candy-coated popcorn had done. He just added a tiny little prize in the box of his candy-coated popcorn. And in the words of Paul Harvey, *"and now you know the rest of the story"*.

The reason I share this story is because I want the youth to understand that special recognitions, and especially rare and limited opportunities, are designed for those who are willing to *do just a little bit more*. Consider blessings that you cannot even begin to imagine; going places that never entered your wildest dream; and people knocking at your door who you never thought you would meet. Such great opportunities are there for you when you are committed to *doing just a little bit more*.

From a biblical perspective, the young lady named Rebekah in our text is a beautiful illustration of how special recognitions, and especially rare and limited opportunities, are bestowed upon those who are willing to *do just a little bit more*.

If you are not familiar with Rebekah, that is okay. Perhaps, she is not as widely known to many as other more famous female Bible characters such as Eve, Sarah, Deborah, Elizabeth, and Mary, the mother of Jesus. Nevertheless, the most fascinating thing about the story of Rebekah is the fact that she was selected to be the wife of Abraham's son, Isaac. This was such a great honor! It meant Rebekah would be a part of the lineage through which the whole world would be blessed. However, that opportunity was presented to Rebekah when Eliezer (Abraham's eldest servant) saw Rebekah with a willingness to *do just a little bit more*.

According to the story, that amazing discovery of Rebekah occurred when Eliezer had arrived at a place called Mesopotamia during the time of the evening in which the women of the city came to the well to draw water. Eliezer had come to Mesopotamia for the sake of finding a wife for Abraham's eldest son whose name was Isaac. Unlike how it is in America, it was the custom and culture of that time for parents to take the responsibility of searching and selecting a wife for their sons. Although it is not custom for our parents to select our spouses, Eliezer's approach for selecting a wife for Isaac is something we should carefully consider.

Eliezer began selecting a wife for Isaac by going to God in prayer. In Genesis 24:13-14 (KJV), Eliezer prayed:

> [13] Behold, I stand *here* by the well of water; and the daughters of the men of the city come out to draw water: [14] And let it come to pass, that the damsel to whom I shall say, Let down the pitcher, I pray thee, that I may drink; and she shall say, Drink, and I will give thy camels drink also: *let the same be* she *that* thou hast appointed for thy servant Isaac; and thereby shall I know that thou hast showed kindness unto my master.

The scripture teaches in Proverbs 3:6 (KJV) — "In all thy ways acknowledge him, and he shall direct thy path." There is no question about this. In choosing one to be your spouse, do as Eliezer did on behalf of Isaac and ask God to direct your path.

Referring back to Eliezer's prayer, it can easily be deducted Eliezer's selection criteria for the woman he would choose to be the wife for Isaac was based on the woman who was willing to *do just a little bit more*. Read the story and you will see that is exactly what Rebekah did. When Rebekah came to the well to draw water and was approached by Eliezer for a drink of water, Rebekah responded to Eliezer's request. But she also *did a little bit more*. She volunteered to get water for Eliezer's ten camels. There was nothing really spectacular about giving water to Eliezer. In their custom, it was expected and required of Rebekah to be hospitable and kind to a stranger. The distinction came when Rebekah offered to get water for Eliezer's ten camels. To offer and to get water for Eliezer's ten camels was a demonstration of Rebekah's willingness to *do just a little bit more*. Furthermore, *doing just a little bit more* just seemed to have been a part of Rebekah's character. Seemingly, in every inquiry and request by Eliezer to Rebekah, she displayed a willingness to *do just a little bit more*. For instance, after asking Rebekah for water, Eliezer asked Rekebah was there room in her father's house for him to dwell. Eliezer only asked for a place to dwell, but Rekebah also offered straw for Eliezer's camels and food for him. She offered Eliezer a little bit more than what he was actually seeking. Upon hearing that, the scripture says that Eliezer bowed his head and worshiped the LORD (Genesis 24:26, KJV).

Because Rebekah was willing to *do a little bit more,* she received the privilege to become the wife of Abraham's son as well as the daughter-in-law of Abraham who is known as the Father of Faith and as the person through which the whole earth would be blessed. Although she was unaware of these things, she positioned herself to be associated with greatness because she was willing to *do a little bit more.*

There is no doubt in my mind that our youth need to be able to embrace opportunities. Special recognitions and opportunities are designed for those who are willing to *do just a little bit more.*

Matt Roloff was regarded as a little person who went to work for Altos Computer Systems. After a time at Altos, Matt Roloff was moved around, and was moved up, until he was basically running the show in his department. To his astonishment, Matt Roloff described himself as being one of the least qualified and least educated employees at Altos; but he was being moved up because he was willing to give a little extra.[2]

Meadowlark Lemon of the Harlem Globetrotters states that when he played as a freshman in Williston Industrial High School of Wilmington, North Carolina against Sam Jones of Laurinburg Institute, who went on to play for the Boston Celtics, that he soon realized that he was not quite ready for high-level basketball. Subsequently, that caused him to work harder than ever before. Meadowlark Lemon said, *"If the coaches told us to run 10 laps around the basketball court, I would run 20. If they said shoot free throws until you sink 10 in a row, I would shoot until I had made 20 in a row. When my teammates called it a day and headed for the showers, I stayed on the court by myself and shot, dribbled, faked, and shot some more."*[3]

The late Rev. Dr. Samuel Dewitt Proctor told a person by the name of Booker that if he wanted to go to school to give his best and be ready for any opportunity that comes.[4] **When you *do just a little bit more,* you are getting yourself ready for opportunities that will come your way.** You do not have to do a whole lot more. You only need to *do just a little bit more* – simply go beyond what is required of you. Nonetheless, there are four things I want us to understand when we make a commitment to *doing just a little bit more.*

First, you will have to do some things alone. It is clear that when Rebekah came to the well she came alone. Jesus taught in Matthew 7:13-14 (KJV), "[13] Enter ye in at the strait gate: for wide is the gate, and broad is the way, that leadeth to destruction, and many there be which go in thereat: [14] Because strait *is* the gate, and narrow *is* the way, which leadeth unto life, and few there be that find it." Do not expect your friends to hang with you when you commit to *doing just a little bit more.*

- Be prepared to read more than what is required of you alone.
- Be prepared to study an extra hour alone.
- Be prepared to think for yourself alone.
- Be prepared to go to the library alone.
- Be prepared to do more than what is required of you alone.

Before he was discovered, it is held that the great saxophone player Grover Washington, Jr. would go on the Brooklyn Bridge in New York alone and play his saxophone every night. The great Byron Pitts, the African-American correspondent for Sixty-Minutes, used to stand in the mirror every day alone practicing as if he was speaking into a camera. Again, Meadowlark Lemon of the Harlem Globetrotters, after playing basketball each day, would alone go and practice the hook shot which made him famous. Even Jesus got alone early in the morning before dawn to pray.

There are some things in life that can only be accomplished alone. In part, the books I have written stem from many hours late at night until early in the morning working alone. So, if I am going to be committed to *doing just a little bit more*, I must also be prepared to do some things alone.

Second, you become a source of inspiration to others. In 2004, I was the speaker at the "6th Annual Recognition & Achievement Day

Program" for the Piney Grove Baptist Church in Hillsborough, North Carolina. The highlight of that event was when a person by the name of Gloria Stewart Brooks was recognized for her accomplishments. Unrelenting applauds flowed from the congregation when her name was called. For you see at the age of 50, Sister Brooks went back to school to obtain her high school diploma. After the program, I talked to Sister Brooks to hear her story. In her story, she conveyed to me that she was inspired to go back to school after her son, at the age of 22, returned to school to get his high school diploma. Sister Brooks shared how her son said to her, "Momma why don't you try it. If I can do it, you can." Being inspired by her son's willingness to *do just a little bit more* for his life, Sister Brooks, through the James Madison High School in Atlanta, Georgia, returned to school to earn her high school diploma while graduating with a 4.0 grade point average.

When we *do just a little bit more*, we become a source of inspiration to others. Others will be encouraged to take on a new challenge when they see someone who is *doing just a little bit more.*

My youngest sister, who was only two years old when our mother died, graduated in 2003 with a doctorate in material science engineering from Tuskegee University. During the pursuit of her degree, she stayed with one of my older sisters in Tuskegee. The older sister said to me at Tonnia's graduation, *"Tonnia taught me how to study."* By *doing just a little bit more,* Tonnia left a great impression on my sister Gail. When you commit to *doing just a little bit more*, you will become a source of inspiration for others. Others will grow up not only wanting to "be like Mike" but they will also want to be like you. They will begin to believe in themselves because they saw you believing in yourself.

Third, in the little bit more that you do, be sure to do it with a blissful, delightful, and enjoyable attitude. Sometimes people *do a little bit more,* but it all goes unnoticed because of their attitude. Nothing can shut some doors for you like an unpleasant attitude. It is not what you do alone that captivates the attention of others in a positive way. Rather, the type of attitude you project in doing what you do will either draw people to you or drive people away from you.

Keith Harrell said, *"The attitude you carry around makes an incredible difference in your life...It determines whether you are on the way or in the way."*

Matt Roloff holds, *"Attitude is something that comes from deep within us ... [it is] a manifestation of a person's level of comfort with God."*

J. Sidlow asked, *"What is the difference between an obstacle and an opportunity?"* His response was: *"Our attitude towards it."*

Rebekah's attitude was astonishing. The attitude she displayed set her apart and made her blazingly attractive. Simply stated, it got Eliezer's attention. For instance, when Eliezer asked Rebekah for some water, Rebekah said, "Drink my lord" showing kindness and respect. But then the text said she hasted, and let down her pitcher upon her hand, and gave him drink. In other words, she did not waste any time responding to Eliezer's request. She did what she did with a very blissful, delightful, and enjoyable attitude. Everything she did in Eliezer's presence was done with a positive and gracious attitude. Eliezer did not ask Rebekah for water for his ten camels. Rebekah asked Eliezer could she draw water also for his camels. In getting water for the camels, the scripture said that Rebekah hasted, emptied her pitcher into the trough, and ran again unto the well to draw water, and drew for all his camels (Genesis 24:18, KJV). The enthusiasm Rebekah displayed in *doing just a little bit more* left an impression on Eliezer. The text says that it left him wondering at her.

Basically, everybody has an okay attitude when they do what they are required to do. But it is a different story when you are being asked to *do a little bit more*. It is even more delightful when you are *doing a little bit more* without being asked to do it. Rebekah had an even better attitude in *doing a little bit more*, when it was neither required nor requested.

Young people, please do not allow your attitudes to prevent you from having golden opportunities. Do not miss experiencing the joys and the rewards of golden opportunities because of your attitude. Always strive to *do a little bit more* with a blissful, delightful, and enjoyable attitude. Rebekah's attitude fascinated Eliezer. It made Eliezer stop and wonder had the Lord made his journey prosperous which leads to my last point.

Fourth, you will stand out. The main thing that made Eliezer recognize Rebekah from the rest of the women who came to the well was her willingness to *do just a little bit more.* When you *do a little bit more*, it will not go unnoticed. People will look for you. I have this saying: *"Do not seek to be in the spotlight. Rather, do little things; and let others put the spotlight on you."* Others will inquire about you when you *do just a little bit more.*

Norman Vincent Peale shares a story in his book, *Positive Thinking,* about a man who moved from Italy and became president of a big hat manufacturing company. When the person came to America, Peale helped him to get a job in a department store in New York City as a hat salesman. This person, whom Peale called John M, was not content with just trying to sell a hat to customers in which he was only hired to do. He also tried to sell two or three different outfits to his customers. Peale wrote the following comments in his book about John:

> *Naturally, a boy like John was noticed. He was different, and different people cannot help but to be noticed. John was favorably noticed by the hat manufacturer. The result, he is today president of a big hat manufacturing organization.*

When you *do a little bit more*, it will be noticed. As with Rebekah, your differences, your uniqueness, and your distinction will be seen. Pay close attention to what Dr. Martin Luther King Jr. said in a speech to a group of students at Barratt Junior High School in Philadelphia. He said if it falls to your lot to be a street sweeper then:

- sweep streets like Michelangelo painted pictures - *[a little bit more]*,
- sweep streets like Beethoven composed music – *[a little bit more]*,
- sweep streets like Leontyne Price sings before the Metropolitan Opera – *[a little bit more]*,
- sweep streets like Shakespeare wrote poetry – *[a little bit more]*,

- sweep streets so well that all the hosts of heaven and earth will have to pause and say: Here lived a great street sweeper who did his job well – *[a little bit more]*.

When you *do a little bit more*, you will stand out and room will be made for you. If you do just a little bit more, then, in the words of Ralph Waldo Emerson, the world will make a beaten path to your door.

And for your confidence, the grace of God dwelling in you will enable you to *do just a little bit more*. For Paul said in I Corinthians 15:10 (KJV), "But by the grace of God I am what I am: and his grace which *was bestowed* upon me was not in vain; but I laboured more abundantly than they all: yet not I, but the grace of God which was with me."

There is a great lesson to be learned from the history of Cracker Jacks. That lesson is clearly displayed throughout our history as African-Americans. Success awaits those who are willing to *do just a little bit more*. Harry Emerson Fosdick said, *"… no man can be used by a great idea without becoming greater himself."*[5] The same is equally so and perhaps, even more, can be said by those who are willing to do just a little bit more. No person can *do just a little bit more* without having just a little bit more (and even more than a little bit more) done for him or her.

So young people, sons and daughters of kings and queens and great achievers, remember no one can *do a little bit more* without having a little bit more (and even more than a little bit more) returned to them. If you do not believe me, then consider:

- Ben Carson: the African-American, who separated Siamese twins joined at the back of their heads.
- Barry C. Black: the first person of color in the nation's history to serve as Chaplin of the U.S. Senate.
- Jackie Robinson: the first African-American to play Major League Baseball.
- Serena and Venus Williams: two African-American women who have turned the tennis world upside down.

- The Tuskegee Airmen: African-American pilots who made unbelievable efforts in World War II.
- Dorothy Dandridge: the first African-American woman nominated for an Academy Award.
- Barack Obama: the first African-American to become President of the United States.

Finally, doing and giving more is the character of our gracious and loving God! He always does more for us than we ask or expect! The cup we bring to God for Him to pour in always runs over. The basket we bring to God for Him to store our blessings always comes back with blessings pressed down, shaken together, and overflowing. The grace God gives us is nothing short of amazing grace! What God has prepared for us is more than our minds can imagine. It says in the scripture, "But as it is written, EYE HATH NOT SEEN, NOR EAR HEARD, NEITHER HAVE ENTERED INTO THE HEART OF MAN, THE THINGS WHICH GOD HATH PREPARED FOR THEM THAT LOVE HIM" (I Corinthians 2:9, KJV).

We may ask to be saved; but God always saves to the utmost because Jesus, the Author and Finisher of our faith, has been given the only name by which humankind can be saved. That honor was bestowed upon him because throughout his life he was willing to *do just a little bit more*. People came to him just to be healed, but he *did a little bit more* - He made them whole. People just wanted their sins to be forgiven; but he *did a little bit more* - He washed away their sins. People just wanted to be loved and appreciated for what they did; but Jesus *did a little bit more* - He loved them unconditionally. To face that cross on Calvary, Jesus *did a little bit more* - He died and was resurrected to be Lord over all. And because Jesus committed his life to *doing just a little bit more*, we now sing, *"All hail the pow'r of Jesus name! Let angels prostrate fall, Bring forth the royal diadem, And crown Him Lord of all."*

2

LEARNING TO SHINE WHEREVER YOU ARE

It really would be great if we could always be in what we consider to be the ideal place. We feel such a place enables us to accomplish and achieve certain goals, while giving us the opportunity to be recognized for what we do. But, what if we are not in such an ideal place? Can we still do well? Dr. Thomas claims that we can do well when our situations are not ideal. He encourages us to learn how to shine wherever we are. In this sermon, he presents some essential principles that will enable us to shine wherever we are. Dr. Thomas advocates that what we really need to shine does not depend upon where we reside; but upon The Essentially Important One who resides within us.

Text: Revelation 1:9-11 (KJV)

[9] I John, who also am your brother, and companion in tribulation, and in the kingdom and patience of Jesus Christ, was in the isle that is called Patmos, for the word of God, and for the testimony of Jesus Christ.

[10] I was in the Spirit on the Lord's day, and heard behind me a great voice, as of a trumpet,

[11] Saying, I am Alpha and Omega, the first and the last: and, What thou seest, write in a book, and send *it* unto the seven churches which are in Asia; unto Ephesus, and unto Smyrna, and unto Pergamos, and unto Thyatira, and unto Sardis, and unto Philadelphia, and unto Laodicea.

All of us have probably heard someone say, and perhaps we all have said it ourselves, "If I were in a different situation or if my circumstances were different, things for me would be completely different and much better." That might be true to a certain extent, but if our present conditions and circumstances never changed, can we still make our dreams come true? Is it still possible for us to *become a shining star exactly where we are?*

I am beginning to believe that the core of many people's frustrations is in their insistence on trying to live in an arena or a lifestyle that does not presently exist for them. God's question to Moses when he was facing the Red Sea was: *"Moses, what do you have in your hand?"*

Chuck Swindoll says, *"To get somewhere else, it's necessary to know where you are presently standing."* Could it be that some are not progressing and shining brightly where they presently are because they are trying to work with things that they do not have, instead of working with the things that they do have?

Many of us probably would never have had the opportunity to enjoy the delicacy of **chitlins (or chitterlings)** if our foreparents had not learned how to take throwaways, which were thrown to them, and create from them something exquisitely delicious.

Nevertheless, the relevant question is, can we *shine wherever we are?* Well, the writing of the Book of Revelation is a very strong indication that "yes, we can".

Most people who are familiar with the Book of Revelation know it as a strange mystical book. But in addition to that, the circumstances, and the place upon which it was written, make it a very phenomenal book. The Book of Revelation was written on an island called Patmos, an unlikely place to write a book. People sentenced to death were often taken to the Isle of Patmos to die a slow death by either starvation, or from a vicious attack by a wild animal. The Isle of Patmos was a barren, rocky and dangerous place. Death was a guaranteed experience if one was left on the Isle of Patmos. Yet, the Lord, from the Isle of Patmos, prepared John to write the Book of Revelation with its symbols and coded language to give the Christian community a vivid picture of how things would be in the future.

Perhaps, one of the most startling things to me about the Book of Revelation is the notion that a book of hope was written from a place of desolation and despair. Though left to die in a place of desolation and despair, John penned an encouraging message of hope to people who may be dwelling in a similar but better situation.

As I pondered John's situation, I had to ask this question: What enables a person to survive and shine under conditions such as the Isle of Patmos? What enables a person to shine like that?

With respect to modern times, how was Beethoven able to write music in spite of being deaf? How could Stevie Wonder play the piano being blind? How was Christy Brown able to write over a thousand letters and four novels with just his left foot? How could Dr. Martin Luther King Jr. write his best letters while being detained in the Birmingham jail? How could the 1995 Miss America, Heather Whitestone, dance to music for talent while being deaf? How could Arnulf Erich Stegmann learn to write and paint with a pencil between his teeth even though he was stricken with polio when he was three years old and lost the use of his hands and arms? How could Barry C. Black, who was raised in the crime, drugs, and poverty infected public housings of Baltimore, Maryland, become the first person of color in the history of the United States to serve as Chaplin of the U.S. Senate?

I raised those questions because I want our youth, regardless of where they are, to know that they can be productive; they can sparkle; they can be distinguished; they can be polished; and they can be brilliant. I want them to know that a beam of light can emanate from their work and personality. I want them to be filled with happiness. I want them to experience joy and love as they matriculate through the developmental years of their lives. Moreover, I want them to have a glow of confidence in their God-given abilities. Simply stated, I want them to be able to *shine, shine, shine, shine wherever they are!*

Our text suggests, at least, four things that we need to understand or do before we will be able to shine wherever we are. Let us consider them.

First, you cannot allow where you are to determine who you are.
One of the things which comes out noticeably clear in our text is that being out on the Isle of Patmos did not change John. The text says in Revelation 1:9 (KJV) — "I John, who also am your brother, and companion in tribulation, and in the kingdom of God and patience of Jesus Christ, was in the isle that is called Patmos, for the word of God, and for the testimony of Jesus Christ."

Where John was did not change who he was. To shine wherever you are, you must be who you are wherever you are. Being who you are wherever you are means that you do not let others define you. Nor do you allow others to determine what you **CAN** do.

God in His grace and goodness has given you what I call the **CAN** power. Youth, I want you to please take note of the concept of **CAN** power.

Now, the **CAN** power enables us to obtain and become. But you must put it to use no matter where you are. For you see, **CAN** power is not based upon where you are. It is within you. Paul noted in Philippians 4:13 (KJV), "I **can** do all things through Christ which strengtheneth me."

In his book, *Gifted Hands*, Ben Carson tells when leaving church one Sunday, he said to his mother that he wanted to be a doctor. Upon hearing him say that, Ben Carson's mother put her hand on Ben Carson's shoulder and said to him, *"If you ask the Lord for something and believe He will do it, then it'll happen."*⁶ Ben Carson then said to his mother, *"I believe I can be a doctor."*⁷ In the words of Paul Harvey, *"and you know the rest of the story"*. Ben Carson became a famous and outstanding doctor who was the lead neurosurgeon of a seventy-member surgical team, the first to separate conjoined twins.

Young people, my heart overflows with joy when I think about what you can become through Christ. Regardless of the complications, the obstacles, the distractions, the agitations, and the disadvantages, you **CAN** succeed because of what you **CAN** do through Christ despite where you are. Through Christ remember God has given you **CAN** power. You **CAN** do all things through Christ which strengthens you. Regardless of how torn your life may be, it **CAN** become whole and complete. Regardless of how discouraged you maybe today with life, you **CAN** have hope for tomorrow. You **CAN** *shine wherever you are* because you know you **CAN** become someone great and you **CAN** do great things through Christ.

Second, what's essential for you to shine is not determined by where you are. I once read an interesting article entitled, "**SUPERKIDS**." Basically, the article was about kids who did extremely well but who were not expected by the experts to do well. The headlines in the article stated, *"No one knows why some children who grow up under horrendous conditions - in homes with abusive, psychotic, or desperately poor parents - seem to develop into extraordinarily competent human beings. In the mystery of why these 'invulnerables' thrive while other breaks, psychologists hope to find clues to optimal human development."*

This is not a criticism, but the psychologists seem not to have understood what is essential for a child to shine. Jessie Jackson said, *"I was born in the slums, but the slums were not born in me."* Again, referring to Ben Carson, of himself he said, *"the exhausted primary neurosurgeon who had devised the plan for the operation was a ghetto kid from the streets of Detroit."*[8]

Please understand, we are neither doomed to everlasting failure, nor is everlasting prosperity our journey because of the conditions into which we were born.

John could write the Book of Revelation on the Isle of Patmos because what was essential for him to write was not determined by where he was. John said I was in the Spirit. What John needed to enable and to encourage him to write was the presence of God. And God is omnipresence. He is everywhere. There was no place that John could have gone or been placed that God was not there. Regardless of where John would have been placed, John would have been on holy ground because the earth is the Lord's. It is not where you are that is of utmost importance; it is God's presence.

My oldest brother has been such an inspiration to his twelve siblings by being an example of excellence, giving, love, determination, humility, and dedication to God and family, as well as other virtues that are essential to a strong, vibrant, and healthy life. One day in a conversation with me, as he was kindly reflecting on the things I had done and was doing, he asked me, *"Would you have ever believed that you would have been able to do what you have done growing up by the side of the railroad track?"* My response to my brother's question was, *"Yes, because God's presence is by the side of the railroad track."*

After saying that, what the Psalmist declared in Psalm 139:7-10 (KJV) rolled into mind for it says, *"⁷ Whither shall I go from thy spirit? or whither shall I flee from thy presence? ⁸ If I ascend up into unto heaven, thou art there: if I make my bed in hell, behold, thou art there. ⁹ If I take the wings of the morning, and dwell in the uttermost parts of the sea; ¹⁰ Even there shall thy hand lead me, and thy right hand shall hold me."*

God's presence is what makes the difference. It is never where you are; nor where you are from.

Eugene Peterson wrote: *"Environment is important, culture is important, history is important. But none of these items is decisive. Place and time are important .... But place and time are not decisive ..... The most important single thing about the people of God is that they are there. They exist. They are .... because God called them out of nothing and made them."*

Even before we made our entrance into the world, God's presence was with us. To Jeremiah, in Jeremiah 1:5, God said, *"Before I formed thee in the belly I knew thee; and before thou camest forth out of the womb I sanctified thee, and I ordained thee a prophet unto the nations."* Then David said in Psalm 139:13 (KJV), *"For thou hast possessed my reins: thou hast covered me in my mother's womb."*

Young people, you have what is essential to do well. You have a brain, a mind, and you have a heart. You only need to use your brain and your mind and be driven by your heart. Not only that, but you also have parents whom God has given to encourage and support you. Truly, they are primarily responsible for your education. As your primary educator, they are in partnership with the school systems to help ensure you receive an adequate education that prepares you for adulthood.

During my work at the United Theological Seminary in Dayton,

Ohio, I met the mother of Mannie Marble who is a professor at Columbia University. Dr. Marble has authored over fifteen books including the book, *Malcolm X*. Interestingly, when I met Dr. Marble, that same week the Madison Time had an article written by him. In that article, Dr. Marble said of his father (James Marble): *"For years, Dad was a full-time student during the day and a factory-maintenance worker on the night shift. He worked two full-time jobs for nearly two decades to make sure that his sons and daughter could attend college and make something more of their lives."*

Young people respect and honor your parents because they are an essential ingredient in helping you *shine where you are*. And if by chance you feel your parents are failing you in this aspect of your life, remember the Bible says in Psalms 27:10 (KJV), "When my mother and my father forsake me, then the LORD will take me up."

Third, to shine wherever you are, you must have discipline. No one reaches high heights without some form of discipline. When you look closely at the text, you will discover that what John experienced, in part, was the result of discipline. The text says that John was in the spirit on the Lord's Day, which suggests that worship was something that John did on the Lord's Day, regardless of where he was. John did not worship because he was on the Isle of Patmos. John worshiped because that was something that he knew to be of great value to his life. Despite where he was, John knew that on the Lord's Day, he needed to worship. Now that is discipline!

Young people, if you want to shine wherever you are, you must practice discipline. Discipline is vitally important for disciples. According to Eddie B. Lane, discipline gives you the ability to live skillfully. But I admire what Camellia William said in a conversation about discipline. She stated that she practiced discipline because of the prize. In other words, if I do certain things there is a prize for doing it.

Young people learn the art of self-discipline. Demand of yourselves that you do certain things without being told because you know they yield great results. Consider even the small things that bring great results. Go to bed early during the school year because you know it helps you to be alert in school. Get up on time and take time to eat a good breakfast before school so you will have the energy to learn. Study, read and do your homework every single school day because you know it will increase your comprehension and earn you good grades and many opportunities will follow. Do not party during the week so you can concentrate on your schoolwork. Retain a level of respect for yourself that will give you possibilities to be among notable people and gain access to respectable places and positions.

Young people, please be disciplined knowing a great prize awaits those who are disciplined. Paul said in Philippians 3:14 (KJV), "I press toward the mark for the prize of the high calling of God in Christ Jesus." To *shine wherever you are*, you must have discipline.

Fourth, you must be attentive and responsive to God's direction. Understandably, there are things we may be asked to do which, on the surface, appear logically impractical or unreasonable for us to do. For instance, it did not seem logically practical for Moses to think that he and the children of Israel could cross the Red Sea, but they did.

It did not seem logically practical for Joshua and the children of Israel to march once around the city of Jericho six straight days; and then on the seventh day, march seven times around the city of Jericho. After the seventh time around the city, the priests were to blow the trumpets. When the people heard the sound of the trumpets, they were told to shout; not knowing that the noise of their shouting would cause the walls of Jericho to fall down flat. Well, the children of Israel did as they were instructed and the walls of Jericho fell down flat to the ground.

Scientifically, it is practically unreasonable to think that a woman can become pregnant and bear a child without any involvement with a man. Based on our human understanding, such a thing is impossible. However, as unreasonable as that may be scientifically, it did happen to a young girl named Mary. She became pregnant with the Savior of the world without the involvement of a man. Nevertheless, it was what Mary said to the angel that helps us to understand why we can still shine when we are being asked to do things which seem impossible based on where we are. To the angel,

Mary said in Luke 1:38 (KJV),"*Behold the handmaid of the Lord; be it unto me according to thy word.*" It is because of what God has declared, that those in Biblical times and in modern times can shine wherever God has placed them.

Writing the Book of Revelation was not work that was brewing in John's heart. It was given to John. We know that because Revelation 1:10-11 (KJV) says:

> [10] I was in the Spirit on the Lord's day, and heard behind me a great voice, as of a trumpet, [11] Saying, I am Alpha and Omega, the first and the last: and, What thou seest, write in a book, and send *it* unto the seven churches which are in Asia; unto Ephesus, and unto Smyrna, and unto Pergamos, and unto Thyatira, and unto Sardis, and unto Philadelphia, and unto Laodicea.

Like other Biblical characters, John was only doing what God instructed him to do. But to do it, John had to be attentive and responsive to the voice of God.

To be attentive to the voice of God, John, for a moment, had to shift his attention from what he was doing and turn to hear the great voice that was behind him. John was out there on the Isle of Patmos alone. Therefore, John could not ignore what he heard as if it was just an ordinary sound. He became attentive to the voice of God. But it was not until John became attentive to the voice of God that God begins to speak to John.

Like Moses, when he led his father-in-law's flock to the far side of the wilderness and came to Horeb, there was a flame of fire in the midst of a bush. The bush, however, was not being consumed. This strange phenomenon caused Moses to turn his attention from what he was doing to seek an understanding of why the bush was not being consumed. When Moses shifted his attention, it was then that God began to speak to Moses.

Young people, to be attentive to the voice of God, for even a moment, you must shift your attention from what you are doing. Set your mind and heart to listen to the voice of God and to hear clearly, without any distraction, the directions God has for your life. Once God's directions are clearly received, you must then follow His directions. Trust God to make a reality all the things He reveals to you. And if you do that, you will be able to *shine wherever you are.*

Young people, there is no doubt in my mind that you can *shine wherever you are.* Nevertheless, please remember to *shine wherever you are,* do not allow where you are to determine who you are; remember what is essential for you to shine is not determined by where you are; remember to practice discipline as a mandatory principle of life; and remember that you must be attentive and responsive to God's directions.

There are some things in life we will never forget. One of the things I will never forget is a story told by Dr. L. Charles Bennett during my first visit to the Hampton Minister Conference in 1987. Dr. Bennett spoke of a day he went home for lunch. To save time, he cut through the back alleys of his neighborhood. As he was running through the alleys, something caught his attention and he was forced to stop. There amidst the filth, garbage, trash, and concrete was a beautiful little flower. Dr. Bennett said he had to stop to ask the flower a question. He asked the flower, *"What in the world are you doing here in this back alley surrounded by filth, garbage, trash and concrete?"* In his vivid imagination, Dr. Bennett said the flower spoke to him and said, *"Oftentimes in life we are not responsible for where we have been placed. Therefore, we have to learn to blossom and grow where we are."*

Young people, we are not always responsible for where we have been placed in life. However, we must still *shine wherever we are.* Yes, be well assured that we can shine wherever we are because ultimately our ability to shine does not rest on us. For as long as we allow the Light from the Lighthouse of Heaven to shine on us, we can *shine wherever we are.* We just have to say: "Shine on me Blessed Son of God. Let the Light from the Lighthouse of Heaven shine on me."

The greatest illustration of one being able to shine regardless of where he was is Jesus. He is God's greatest wonder of mankind shining in the most gruesome situation at Calvary which was no match even for the Isle of Patmos. There at Calvary stood an old rugged cross upon which Jesus was crucified bearing our sins before God. Yet, on that old rugged cross, Jesus was able to shine. He shined so bright that His brightness dimmed the sun. He shined so brilliantly that the sun became covered with darkness that covered the face of the earth. Yes, Jesus shined so bright, with such great illuminating power, that He is able to save sinners like us. Because He has shined for us, we are now positioned to shine for Him wherever we are. Thank God that Jesus was able to shine to give us grace to *shine wherever we are*! Thank God! AMEN.

3

SLUMBERING AND SLEEPING AT THE WRONG TIME

The intention of this sermon is to encourage youth to not waste their developmental years. These years are designed to prepare them to be ready to take advantage of opportunities that will come their way as they grow into adulthood. Dr. Thomas characterizes the failure to prepare as slumbering and sleeping at the wrong time.

Text: Matthews 25:1-13 (KJV)

¹ Then shall the kingdom of heaven be likened unto ten virgins, which took their lamps, and went forth to meet the bridegroom.

² And five of them were wise, and five *were* foolish.

³ They that *were* foolish took their lamps, and took no oil with them:

⁴ But the wise took oil in their vessels with their lamps.

⁵ While the bridegroom tarried, they all slumbered and slept.

⁶ And at midnight there was a cry made, Behold, the bridegroom cometh; go ye out to meet him.

⁷ Then all those virgins arose, and trimmed their lamps.

⁸ And the foolish said unto the wise, Give us of your oil; for our lamps are gone out.

⁹ But the wise answered, saying, *Not so*; lest there be not enough for us and you: but go ye rather to them that sell, and buy for yourselves.

[10] And while they went to buy, the bridegroom came; and they that were ready went in with him to the marriage: and the door was shut.

[11] Afterward came also the other virgins, saying, Lord, Lord, open to us.

[12] But he answered and said, Verily I say unto you, I know you not.

[13] Watch therefore, for ye know neither the day nor the hour wherein the Son of man cometh.

SIDE NOTE:

While you're asleep, every system in your body is being fine-tuned, reset, cleaned up and restored to its optimal operating mode by an army of molecular troubleshooters. New things you have learned are being processed, memories are being organized and stored, and the immune system is building a new contingent of natural killer cells to fight off battalions of infectious agents. Growth hormones are being produced to repair damaged tissues (in adults) or build new tissues (in children) and to block the corrosive effects of stress. When you sleep well, you're in peak operating condition.

How surprised we would be to think about the number of things we think we need but we can actually live without! I am amazed how quickly we forget that some things the commercial industry insists we must have, we once lived without; and we fared extremely well without those things.

Before Air Jordan's, I did okay on the basketball court with a pair of Converse All Stars. I am not complaining, but I believe dinner tasted a little better before the invasion of the microwave. Definitely, the smartphone is a jewel; but Superman did fine changing in a telephone booth.

I admit new inventions have their advantages. I am just suggesting that there are many things we can live without that we think we must have. On the other hand, there are some things that we cannot live without, and sleep is one of those things.

Sleep is one of life's non-replaceable essentials, just like air, food, and water. Can you imagine how we would be if we could not sleep when our bodies are tired? I really do not want to know. Just a little sleep sometimes is the best way to get through certain things.

- Sometimes the best medicine for pain is just a little sleep.
- Often the best form of relaxation is just a little sleep.
- Perhaps a good way to solve complex matters is by just getting a little sleep.
- In many cases, the best form of stress relief is just a little sleep.
- And so often the best comfort for a troubled mind is just a little sleep.

Without question, it is a tremendous blessing to be able to sleep. Sleep fine-tunes our bodies to process new things we have learned. Sleep causes the growth of hormones to repair damaged tissues in adults and builds new tissues in children. I think we must conclude, without a doubt, that sleep is good for all of us.

Now, despite how good of a friend sleep is to us and for us, sleep can be one of our worst enemies if we slumber and sleep at the wrong time. There are times when it is just the wrong time to sleep. For instance:

- When it is time to be at work, and you are still in bed, you are slumbering and sleeping at the wrong time.
- When it is time to be studying for an exam, and you are still in bed, you are slumbering and sleeping at the wrong time.
- When it is time to be at your bus stop for school, and you are still in bed, you are slumbering and sleeping at the wrong time.
- When it is time to be at an important appointment, and you are still in bed, you are slumbering and sleeping at the wrong time.

As good as sleep is to us and for us, if we slumber and sleep at the wrong time, sleep can also be our biggest enemy, bringing us great misfortunes and missed opportunities.

I do not mean to be judgmental, but the relaxation of slumbering and sleeping is one thing that seems to be misused by the youth in every generation. Nothing is inherently wrong with relaxation if it is not slumbering and sleeping at the wrong time. Sometimes what makes a thing bad is not what is being done, but the time in which it is being done.

For this reason, I turned to the parable told by Jesus about ten virgins, waiting to meet the bridegroom to better understand the time when it is wrong to slumber and sleep. To do this, it is necessary to understand what a wedding was like in Palestine during the setting of this parable told by Jesus.

A great way to understand anything is to begin with its uniqueness. One of the unique things about a wedding in Palestine was the uncertainty of the time when the bridegroom would appear. Unlike our culture, no one really knew when the bridegroom would come. The bridegroom could come early in the morning, midday, in the evening, or even in the middle of the night. Regardless of the time of the arrival of the bridegroom, the bridal party was required to be ready to go out into the streets to meet him. To know if he was near, it was required of the bridegroom to send a man into the streets shouting, "*Behold the bridegroom is coming.*"

Now, if the bridegroom came at night, the invited guests were required to meet the bridegroom with a lightened torch or lamp. Without a lightened lamp or torch, you were not allowed in the streets to meet the bridegroom nor allowed to enter the bridegroom's house. Unfortunately, when the bridegroom's doors were shut, no one was allowed to enter the ceremony. So, when Jesus spoke about ten virgins who went forth to meet the bridegroom, his audience understood what the ten virgins had to do to be able to meet the bridegroom regardless of the time he would arrive. This was basically the general concept of a wedding in Palestine.

It is interesting how a group of people may be similar and different in responding to a common situation. Such was the case with the cast in this parable. They were all virgins; but five were wise and five were foolish. Could the distinction between the wise and foolish be their preparation? It is wise to prepare for things just in case certain things happen. It is not wise to know cold weather is going to come and not prepare for it.

I have learned when you least expect something; it is probably going to happen. It was probably not expected, but the bridegroom was delayed. When something is delayed, there is the tendency for people to slumber and sleep. People flying on a plane do it all the time. Many often sleep on the plane while waiting to arrive at their destination. Thus, the wise and the foolish virgins slept while waiting for the bridegroom. When the bridegroom finally arrived, it was at midnight. Therefore, to meet the bridegroom in the street, they had to go out with a lightened lamp or a torch.

Hearing that the bridegroom was near, both the wise and the foolish virgins woke up and trimmed their lamps. However, the foolish virgins had a problem. Their oil ran out. Therefore, they were not able to meet the bridegroom. Consequently, they were unable to participate and were unable to enjoy a wonderful event. They missed it because of slumbering and sleeping when they had not prepared for the known possibilities of the future. What a lesson to learn from the five foolish virgins about the misfortune that comes with slumbering and sleeping at the wrong time.

Some things to me are so troubling – especially opportunties which are missed due to idleness. I know our youth wants to be able to enjoy and reach certain goals. Knowing this, we must make sure our youth do not slumber and sleep during the developmental years of their lives. Do not let anyone mislead you. A successful future to a large extent is determined by what we do during the time we are developing our minds.

Mike Shanahan, once head coach of the Denver Broncos and the Washington Redskins, states in his book, <u>Think Like a Champion</u>: *"The difference between someone who is successful and someone who isn't is not talent. It is about preparation. Preparation enables people to move ahead, stay ahead, and live ahead. Without preparation, you're asking for a passport for failure."* Therefore, let us make sure we are not applying for a passport to failure by slumbering and sleeping at the wrong time.

So, the relevant question is: What do I need to be aware of to make sure that I am not slumbering and sleeping at the wrong time? Please, do not misunderstand me. There is nothing wrong with slumbering and sleeping. It is a natural activity to slumber and sleep. There is nothing wrong with having fun, joking around, and playing games as a child, preteen, teenager, and young adult. But why was it the wrong time for the five foolish virgins to slumber and sleep while they waited for the bridegroom? Well, let us consider three lessons from the parable to encourage us to avoid slumbering and sleeping at the wrong time.

<u>First, they had not done anything beyond what was required for them to do.</u> The parable began by saying, "Then shall the kingdom of heaven be likened unto ten virgins, which took their lamps, and went to meet the bridegroom." Notice initially, there is no distinction made among the ten virgins. They all took lamps. They all knew that if the bridegroom came during the night, they had to have a lightened lamp. Furthermore, they all knew that for their lamps to burn they needed to have oil in their lamps. Putting oil in their lamps was not a thoughtful decision that they made. That action was required of them. If their lamps were going to burn, they had to put oil in them. To bring extra oil in a container was a thoughtful and conscientious decision made by the five wise virgins. The five wise virgins were prepared because they did more than what was required of them.

If you are only doing what is required of you, you are slumbering and sleeping at the wrong time. Those who excel in their professions always do more than what is required of them. There are no brownie points for going to school. Attending school is something every young person must do. The law of the land forces young people to go to school. But a student is only sleeping at the wrong time if he or she is not strongly seeking to learn while in school. Some might disagree but a student is only slumbering at the wrong time if he or she is merely at school and not advancing.

A professor once told a group of students: "Tell your teachers the answers they want to hear and the answers that they need to know." When we only do that which is required of us, we are slumbering and sleeping at the wrong time. We must do just a little bit more.

Second, they had not prepared themselves for the just-in-case scenario. Here again, all ten virgins brought lamps. This was an indication that all ten virgins knew the bridegroom could come at night. Now the lamps held enough oil to burn for an hour and a half. The five virgins that were classified as being wise brought extra oil in a container in case waiting for the bridegroom extended beyond an hour and a half. The five foolish virgins did not prepare for this situation.

But the parable says that while the bridegroom tarried, they all slumbered and slept. The bridegroom, however, did not come until midnight. The bridegroom came at an unlikely time. Although the bridegroom did not come until midnight, the five wise virgins could rest or sleep peacefully because they had prepared themselves to meet the bridegroom in the event he came at an unlikely time. On the other hand, because the five foolish virgins had not prepared for this situation, it was the wrong time for them to slumber and sleep.

Life continuously teaches us that things do not always turn out the way we may have planned them. Things happen beyond our control.

We all should plan; but only God has control of what will occur. Therefore, in preparing ourselves, we must prepare ourselves for unfavorable, undesirable, or unexpected situations.

A car only needs four tires to be driven safely. But we have a spare tire just in case one of the tires goes flat. Like a tire on a car, we all need to understand that things in life at any time can go flat on us. Therefore, we must be prepared for such things so that we can continue to move forward, onward, and upward with our lives.

Young people, please consider the following as examples of things to take careful heed to in preparing for life:

- If you are an athlete, be sure to prepare yourself in case you do not make it to the next level, whether high school, college, or professional leagues.
- Young ladies, please prepare yourself in case you do not marry someone who is wealthy and famous.
- To all, please prepare yourself for not winning the lottery.
- Each of us must prepare ourselves for the way technology will change the job market.
- To those of us who are minorities, we must prepare ourselves for the day when Affirmative Action is altered as we know it; or when it is completely abandoned.
- For those who have special skills for music, art, and theater, you too must be prepared in case you never receive an invitation to Broadway, the Apollo, Carnegie Hall, Dancing with the Stars, American Idol, or America's Got Talent.
- To those who expect to ride the coat-tails of others, remember that you too must prepare yourselves in the event those who made it to prominent positions lack the resources required to bring you up with them.

Young people, please hear me. Be prepared to do other things than what you have planned to do; else, you become like the five foolish virgins. In other words, you will be slumbering and sleeping at the wrong time.

Third, they had not taken personal responsibility for their future endeavors. When the cry was made - *Behold the bridegroom cometh* - both the wise and the foolish virgins woke up and trimmed their lamps. But the oil in the lamps of the five foolish virgins had gone out. What the five foolish virgins said to the five wise virgins is an indication that the five foolish virgins had not personally taken responsibility for their potential future needs. They said in Matthew 25:8 (KJV), "...give us of your oil; for our lamps are gone out." Another translation is: *"Our torches are extinguishing themselves."*

The translation indicates that the five foolish virgins blamed the lamps for their predicament. They never confessed they had been irresponsible. They did not acknowledge their personal failure to adequately prepare themselves. Instead, they blamed the extinguishing of their torches on others. They blamed others for their demise.

I know discrimination, racism, and unfairness are still very much a problem for African-Americans. Nevertheless, we cannot blame all our problems on discrimination, racism, and unfairness. We must personally take responsibility for our future endeavors. We cannot expect other people to take responsibility for our education. We cannot continue to blame discrimination, racism, and unfairness as reasons we do not have certain programs in our communities. We must take personal responsibility for ourselves and for our future.

There are some things we have that are only enough for ourselves. The five wise virgins said to the five foolish virgins in Matthew 25:9 (KJV): "... *Not so*; lest there be not enough for us and you ..." Thus, there are some things we just cannot borrow. There are some things we must get on our own.

Young people, you cannot borrow things that you yourself must develop for yourself during your youth so that you can have a productive life. Consider for example these things that you must have for yourself:

- You cannot borrow someone else's reading ability.
- You cannot borrow someone else's writing ability.
- You cannot borrow someone else's thinking ability.

- You cannot borrow someone else's good behavior.
- You cannot borrow someone else's character.

If you do not have these things, you will have to do like the five foolish virgins - go and obtain those things for yourself. If you have not personally taken the responsibility for your future endeavors, you are slumbering and sleeping at the wrong time.

Young people, you are dear, beautiful, and gifted! Therefore, do not slumber and sleep at the wrong time. Do not be like the five foolish virgins. Let it not be said that you are unprepared for the opportunities knocking at your door. Let it not be said your misfortunes are due to a lack of being prepared.

Do not prepare too late. Some doors are only opened once. If we are not prepared to enter them when they are open, those opportunities may never be opened to us again.

When the five foolish virgins eventually got oil for their lamps, as Dr. Walter Thomas would say, *"they were one moment too late."* The doors were shut. The opportunity had passed by them to go inside to be part of the wedding ceremony.

My young brothers and sisters, as you enjoy your youth, please do not slumber and sleep at the wrong time. Make sure you are getting prepared to take advantage of the opportunities that will come your way one day in the future. If you are not prepared, doors that are open to others will be closed to you.

This sermon is not only for youth. It is for all of us. I say this because at the end of this parable, Jesus warns us as follows in Matthew 25:13 (KJV): "Watch therefore, for ye know neither the day nor the hour wherein the Son of man cometh."

The return of Jesus is sure to come. One day He will come back for His church. Therefore, we do not want to be found slumbering and sleeping at the wrong time. When Jesus comes back for His church, those who are not prepared will be left behind to enter into eternal damnation.

Our foreparents understood the importance of being prepared for Christ's coming. They constantly talked about being ready when Jesus comes. They would say that every eye shall see him. His feet are going to strike Mount Zion. They believed so dearly that Christ was coming back until they wrote songs that would constantly remind them of His coming. They wrote praise songs such as the following:

- *You better mind how you talk, you better mind what you are talking about because you got to give an account at the judgment; you better mind.*
- *Be ready when he comes, for he is coming again so soon. Don't let him catch you with your work undone, for he is coming again so soon.*
- *I'll be standing at the station with my ticket in my hand.*
- *Get oil in your vessel; keep your lamp trimmed and burning; be ready when the bridegroom comes!!!!!!!!!!!!!!!!!!!!!!*

If Christ came today, would you be ready to meet Him?

4

A Lesson from Balaam: Learning to Listen to Those Who See What You Do Not See

It is important to make right decisions. This is critical, especially if we knew what was ahead of us down the road of life. Unfortunately, we do not. In many instances, there are encounters down the road of life that we do not see, but others do. To avoid many hurts, misfortunes, losses, and painful experiences, it is an imperative for our youth to listen to those who see things down the road of life that they do not see. In this sermon, Dr. Thomas, in an extremely dramatic fashion, shows the blessings of listening to good advice from good advisors. He helps us to understand key characteristics of those we should listen to who see things we have not seen.

Text: Number 22:28-35 (KJV)

[28] And the Lord opened the mouth of the ass, and she said unto Balaam, What have I done unto thee, that thou hast smitten me these three times?

[29] And Balaam said unto the ass, Because thou hast mocked me: I would there were a sword in mine hand, for now would I kill thee.

[30] And the ass said unto Balaam, *Am* not I thine ass, upon which thou hast ridden ever since *I was* thine unto this day? was I ever wont to do so unto thee? And he said, Nay.

[31] Then the Lord opened the eyes of Balaam, and he saw the angel of the Lord standing in the way, and his sword drawn in his hand: and he bowed down his head, and fell flat on his face.

[32] And the angel of the LORD said unto him, Wherefore hast thou smitten thine ass these three times? behold, I went out to withstand thee, because *thy* way is perverse before me:

[33] And the ass saw me, and turned from me these three times: unless she had turned from me, surely now also I had slain thee, and saved her alive.

[34] And Balaam said unto the angel of the LORD, I have sinned, for I know not that thou stoodest in the way against me: now therefore, if it displease thee, I will get me back again.

[35] And the angel of the LORD said unto Balaam, Go with the men: but only the word that I shall speak unto thee, that thou shalt speak. So Balaam went with the princes of Balak.

When it comes to learning, we are inclined to listen to people who have become successful in some particular enterprise or endeavor. We tend to do that for the sake of trying to discover their means for success and to see if it can be applied for our success. Because of his success in real estate, "when E.F. Hutton speaks everybody listens". If Oprah Winfrey, because of her success, were invited to speak to an assembly, there would be standing room only. There would likely be hundreds of people outside waiting to see if they could possibly make their way into an already over-crowded assembly to hear Oprah Winfrey speak.

We are naturally and mentally willing to listen to people who we perceive to be successful. We are interested in seeing if what they have to offer can help us to be successful with our enterprise or endeavor.

On the other hand, I also believe that we can learn and gain valuable lessons from people who made ill-advised decisions which turned out to be unprofitable for their lives. Dwight Gooden, who became the youngest pitcher ever to win the CY Young Award at the age of twenty, became addicted to drugs which in turn threatened his career and his life. He shared in his book, *Heat*, how after hearing the story of a former drug addict named Ron Dock something changed in his life. Of Ron Dock, Dwight Gooden wrote, *"Every day, Ron Dock preached the same lesson, until it became cemented in my head: change the people, places, and things that feed your addiction. Change your surroundings; stay away from bars; cut off friends, your enablers. Turn your back on them, even if it breaks your heart."*[9]

Surely, we can learn from people who made ill-advised decisions that turned out to be unprofitable for their lives. Therefore, with that in mind, I thought it would be good for us, especially for the youth, to have someone teach us a valuable lesson for life that came as a result of an ill-advised decision. It is for this reason I have asked a person from the Old Testament named Balaam to come and share his story with us. To make room now for Balaam, I am going to step out of the way and give him this moment.

Hello to all, especially to our youth. My name is Balaam. The meaning of my name may not be very impressive to you, so I will keep it concealed. Now if you have never heard of me, you can learn something about me in the Old Testament Book called Numbers in Chapters 22-24.

Without any pretense, it is incredibly humbling and rewarding for me to share my story with you. I am not bragging but I am very humbled by the fact God used me to withhold a nation that was trying to bring harm to the children of Israel. This happened during the time when the children of Israel pitched their tents in the land of Moab during their journey to the Promised Land.

Living in America, you know that there are numerous rewarding things in life that one can do. But I say without any reservation or hesitation that there is nothing more humbling and rewarding than having the opportunity to be used by God according to His grace and mercy.

I say this because the opportunity God gave me almost never happened. That is because I refused to listen and adhere to someone who saw something down the road that I did not see. It is because of that, everywhere I go, I try to teach a lesson, especially to the youth on how to listen to those who see things coming which they cannot and perhaps do not see.

Let me tell you a secret. You can save yourself a tremendous amount of hardship, agony, frustration, pain, losses, setbacks, and many painful tears if you learn to listen to people. Much more, please listen to those who see things coming that you have not yet come to realize, recognize, or understand.

Let me share an incident in my life to help you better understand what I am saying. You can easily follow what I am about to share by reading The Book of Numbers, Chapter 22.

At any rate, there was a person by the name of Balak. He was King of Moab. He sent for me to curse the children of Israel who had come and were dwelling in the land of Moab and Balak became afraid of them. I had gained the reputation that I had the power to bless people and the power to curse people. Because of this reputation, Balak sent a delegation of princes to me. They came to pay me to place a curse upon the children of Israel so that Balak might be able to drive the children of Israel out of the land of Moab.

Strangely, that night the LORD came to me and told me not to go with the delegation, and not to curse the people I was being asked to curse because this people were blessed of God. Therefore, I refused the offer and payment from Balak's delegation.

Well, on the contrary, Balak sent back to me another delegation that was more honorable than the first delegation. They came with a much larger payment. In addition, Balak offered to do whatever I would ask them to do if I would just curse the children of Israel.

I must admit Balak's second offer sounded quite intriguing. However, I told this second delegation that even if Balak offered me his house full of silver and gold, I would not go beyond the word of the LORD my God.

Well, I do not know what I was thinking. I had the delegation to stay overnight to see whether the LORD had something else to tell me. Believe it or not, during that night God talked with me again. God told me, "If the men come to call thee, rise up, *and* go with them, but yet the word which I shall say unto thee, that shalt thou do."

So, when the morning came, I saddled my donkey and went with the delegation of princes from Moab, but God's anger was kindled against me. God's anger was probably kindled against me because of greed. What can I say?

Nonetheless, as we traveled to Moab, there was an angel of the LORD standing down the road with a sword drawn to use on me that I did not see. However, the donkey I was riding saw the angel of the LORD with the sword drawn in his hand. My donkey left the road and went off into the field attempting to avoid the angel; but I hit my donkey to get it back on the road.

Now the angel of the LORD, whom I never saw, went and stood farther down the road where the road had become narrow because it was placed between two vineyards with a stone wall on each side. Again, my donkey saw the angel and moved close to the side of one of the walls to avoid the angel. As a result, my foot was crushed against the wall. Oh, did that hurt! Therefore, I hit my donkey again to get it back on the road.

With that, I just knew we would be on our way. But the angel of the LORD, whom I did not see, went down the road and stood in a place where there was no room at all on either side to pass.

This part of the story kind of brings tears to my eyes. My donkey, who saw that angel of the LORD down the road in a spot with his sword drawn in his hand in which there was no room at all on either side to pass, just stopped and laid down. I then became so angry with my donkey that I pulled out my stick and began to beat my donkey brutally with it. Because I did not see what my donkey saw down the road, little did I know that my donkey was only trying to save my life.

As you know, God can do some amazing things to get our attention. After I had beaten my donkey three different times, God gave my donkey the power to talk to me. You can read the conversation I had with my donkey in Numbers 22:28-30.

Unfortunately, I did some crazy and ill-advised things on this journey. However, I am so glad I listened to my donkey. I did not take the position that a donkey could not tell me anything. Neither did I ask what does a donkey know?

I am glad I understood that just because someone may not be as you are, or have certain advantages, benefits, exposures, fortunes, privileges, and opportunities, that such does not mean that person is not capable of sharing something with you to help you in life.

You will be surprised the different means that God can use to teach us. People think that when parents buy their children a puppy or a dog, they are only giving their children a pet. Sometimes parents buy their children a puppy or a dog so the animal may teach the children loyalty and obedience. Yes indeed, animals can be used to teach us.

I must admit that it was after the conversation with my donkey that the LORD opened my eyes to see the angel of the LORD standing in the way with a sword drawn in his hand.

After I saw that, there was nothing I could say. All I could do was fall down and throw my face into the ground. But this is what really opened my mind to how important it is for us to listen to those who see things down the road that we do not see. The angel of the LORD told me that if my donkey had not turned aside those three times, my life would have been taken and the life of my donkey would have been spared.

Of course, before becoming the aged man I am now, I too was once in a youthful state of being. As a result, I know sometimes it seems as if adults are mean. Sometimes it seems like your parents, other adult family members, the mothers and the fathers of the church, and even your pastor are withholding things from you that you insist on having and think you should have. Nevertheless, you must understand that they see things down the road that you do not yet see.

The disease called AIDS often takes years to develop. Thus, it is called *le poison lent*, which means slow poison. The failure to listen to those who see things down the road that you do not see is like AIDS - slow poison. It may take years to see the effects, but the failure to listen to those who see things down the road that you do not see can be viewed as slow poison.

Quickly let me share with you three reasons I should have listened or adhered to the behavior of my donkey. I might also add that you may find these three reasons helpful to encourage you to listen to those who are close to you who see things down the road that you do not see.

First, I should have understood the relationship that existed between my donkey and me. I would be the first to instruct you to be careful in taking advice from people that you do not know. I am quite sure you were taught never to take advice from a stranger.

For example, Michael Vick, you perhaps know him better than I do. *"In a span of four years, [Michael Vick] went from being the NFL's highest-paid player to an imprisoned ex-player filing for bankruptcy."*[10] Michael Vick blamed part of his financial wreck to allowing people to handle his investments that he did not personally know.

But in my situation, my donkey was an animal that belonged to me. This was a specimen that had carried me around for years. I had been riding on its back. I had been a load on its shoulders for years. My donkey never before went against me. As a matter of fact, my donkey had made life easier for me. While advising me, I failed to take into consideration the relationship that existed between me and the animal that had been carrying me around for years.

To the youth, I say, never forget and always remember the relationship that your parents have with you. I cannot express to you how wonderful it is to have someone caring for you. Even before you knew yourself, they were taking care of you. They do things for you that very few people would even consider doing. The sacrifices they make for you are signs of their love for you. Cherish the relationship you have with your parents and others who are close to you. Listen carefully to them because they most likely see things you cannot see.

Secondly, I should not have misinterpreted the hard resistance or the hard time I experienced. You are aware of Ben Carson, the African-American that performed the first successful surgery to separate Siamese twins who were joined at the back of the head. Did you know that when he and his family moved back to Detroit, Michigan from Boston, Massachusetts, entering the fifth grade in Detroit from Boston, he was ranked the lowest in his class? His classmates nicknamed him, "dummy."

After seeing how poorly he was doing in school, Ben Carson's mother made him and his brother read two books a week. They were only allowed to watch three shows a night on TV. They likely felt their mother was being too hard on them. But Ben Carson went from being ranked the lowest in the class to becoming ranked the highest in the class when he got to the seventh grade. What seemed to have been a hard time turned out to be something very profitable for Ben Carson down the road, many years later in his life.

I should have known that the hard time my donkey was putting me through was for my good. And I am so glad that my donkey gave me a hard time for it saved my life.

Young people, you should not misinterpret things that appear to be hard that are given to you by your parents and others who care for you. Today, the teachers I have come to admire most are those who gave me what appeared to have been a hard time. They saw some things down the road that I did not see. To prepare me for those things, they had to take me through things that seemed hard, difficult, and unreasonable to me.

Let me advise you to be careful and do not misinterpret people making things easy for you as always being in your best interest. People who genuinely care for you will always challenge you to be the best you can be. They will present things to you that are good for you even if it means you must do things that may seem hard at first for you.

Third, I should understand that I will never see it all. I was so insistent on going to Moab to meet Balak. Unfortunately, I never saw the angel of the LORD on the road with a sword drawn in his hand. I did not see the angel the first time. I did not see the angel the second time on that narrow strip of the road. Nor did I see the angel the last time when we could not go around the angel on either side. But I insisted that we continue down that road even though I did not see everything.

Young people of today, it is no question that you are extremely intelligent. Yet, the most intelligent person in the world cannot see it all.

In the America's armed services or military, when one misses a promotion, one can be placed in a category called "Fully Qualified but Not Selected." That says to me that in life, you can have it all, but not necessarily be it all. There is always more to be added to our experiences. There are places we have not yet gone and experiences we have not yet had. Consider for example these things:

- There are things you have not yet learned, experienced or seem.
- There are places you have not seen or heard of.
- There are people with great minds, skills, and talents yet to be discovered.
- There are so many things about life and about this world that are yet not understood.

And because we have not seen it all, we need to listen to those who see things down the road that we are yet to see.

I know that I have taken a lot of your time and I need to bring my discourse to a close. Before I close let me quickly share two things with you. First, you can always repent when you realize that you have failed to listen to those who see things that you do not see. When I realized what I had done I fell on my face and repented for what I had done. The LORD forgave me and gave me another chance.

Lastly, I want to recommend to you Someone you need who is able to help you all the days of your life. Your parents, your close relatives, your mothers and fathers in Christ, your sisters and brothers in Christ, and your pastor want to help you see things you cannot see. The problem is that they can only go but so far. You need Someone who can show you and help you down the road of life until the road comes to an end.

The person I want to recommend to you is the Lord Jesus Christ. He can lead you all the way. As a matter of fact, He can lead you all the way from earth to heaven. He can lead you safely and successfully all the way to glory. Trust Him; and He will do for you far more than I can tell.

There is a story Howard Thurman told about a young man who came to him with tears flowing down his cheeks. The tears came as a quiet flood upon his face after hearing Thurman preach a sermon in the Anglican Cathedral in Madras, India. The young man came up to Thurman and said to him, *"You did my Master wrong. It was a terrible thing. You preached your entire sermon and not one time did you call my Savior by name, not one time."*[11] Thurman replied, *"...did my words seem to you true to His teaching? Did you sense His Spirit in our midst?"*[12] The young man responded: *"Yes, but this is not the point. You did not call Him by name. And it is important that His name be lifted up that He might draw all men unto Him."*[13]

So, I recommend the Lord Jesus Christ to you Young People. He is more than able to lead, guide and carry you through life. Remember simply call His Name and ask Him to order your steps every day. Please call His Name and ask Him to lead you through school, through college, through the selection of your career, through courtship, through the selection of your mate, through whatever you desire to do. In all your ways, acknowledge Him and He will direct your paths. If He leads you, He will make you happy and give you a wonderful place and position in life. Be well assured He will do for you more than I can tell. Keep calling His Name and watch Him do things for you — things which eyes have not seen, ears have not heard, and which never entered your hearts.

God bless you Young People. Amen.

5

DAVID'S ARMAMENT AGAINST GOLIATH:
A GOOD SENSE OF SELF-WORTH

What is it that prevents us from allowing ourselves to be defiled? Dr. Thomas provides an answer to this question in this sermon. Through the story of David and Goliath, Dr. Thomas shows that a good sense of self-worth prevents us from being defiled. From the surface, David was no match for Goliath. However, as Dr. Thomas emphasizes, it was David's good sense of self-worth that motivated him to fight and to defeat Goliath. This sermon stresses to the youth the importance of having a good sense of self-worth to give them the fortitude to withstand those vices that seek to defile and to destroy them.

Text: I Samuel 17:48-51 (KJV)

[48] And it came to pass, when the Philistine arose, and came and drew nigh to meet David, that David hasted, and ran toward the army to meet the Philistine.

[49] And David put his hand in his bag, and took thence a stone, and slang *it*, and smote the Philistine in his forehead, that the stone sunk into his forehead; and he fell upon his face to the earth.

[50] So David prevailed over the Philistine with a sling and with a stone, and smote the Philistine, and slew him; but *there was* no sword in the hand of David.

[51] Therefore David ran, and stood upon the Philistine, and took his sword, and drew it out of the sheath thereof, and slew him, and cut off his head therewith. And when the Philistines saw their champion was dead, they fled.

There are certain Biblical stories that easily find a resting place in our memories. The story of David and Goliath is one of those stories.

I am quite sure many people have heard the story of David and Goliath. David, a little shepherd boy, defeated Goliath - a mighty warrior over nine feet tall - with a slingshot and a stone. Although that is perhaps the most fascinating thing about the story, I want us to consider what enabled David to have the audacity to consider fighting Goliath.

Again, may I repeat, David used a slingshot and a stone to defeat Goliath. David reached into his bag and used one of the five smooth stones that he had gotten from a brook. He slung the stone at Goliath. The stone hit Goliath in the forehead and broke his skull. Subsequently, Goliath fell face down on the ground. Now I am not minimizing David's miraculous defeat of Goliath with his sling and stone. However, there is more to the story than what meets the eye.

From this most beautiful and spectacular story, I find an interest in what motivated David to take on the challenge of fighting Goliath. I contend what is extremely important, especially for youth, in this story is not the stone and the sling which David used to defeat Goliath, but rather what gave David the courage, the fortitude, and the nerve to consider fighting a person like Goliath. This is where the story becomes truly meaningful, relevant, and significant for young people and others too.

Let us remember that Goliath was a giant and was over nine feet tall. He was a champion and a skillful warrior. On the other hand, David was just a little ruddy shepherd boy without any real warfare experience at all. Realistically, what could a shepherd boy do against a skillful warrior like Goliath?

I am sure there were other skilled warriors in the Israelite army who were better trained to fight against Goliath. However, no one from the Israelite army volunteered to fight Goliath, not even one of David's three brothers who were members of the Israelite army. Therefore, I am curious to know what David possessed, or what possessed David, to take on the challenge to fight Goliath? Whatever it was, it was enormously powerful; and it caused David to step forward and take on what appeared to be an unrealistic challenge.

My curiosity is driven by the fact that giants are still with us today. At some point in time, our children will have to contend with a giant. Understandably, today's giants may not appear in the same form as in the days of David. Nevertheless, the nature of giants remains the same, and they are all around us.

According to David's description of Goliath, a giant is anything that defies us or brings reproach upon our lives. The words "defy" and "reproach" in the Hebrew means to cast scorn and guilt for the purpose of destroying one's character. Actually, David never addressed Goliath according to his size. David addressed Goliath according to his behavior. As such, David said, *"...who is this uncircumcised Philistine that defies the army of the living God."* Therefore, a giant is not necessarily something that is big, huge, or large; but a giant is anything that can devastate, scorn, offend, and severely harm our character. Consequently, giants can be things such as drugs and substance abuse; hanging out with the wrong people and in the wrong places; being irresponsible; bad choices and decisions; failures to develop the mind; and the lack of appreciation for decency. These are all examples or forms of giants that can harm your character which is a very important possession.

Our character is a rare commodity. We only get one. Unfortunately, unlike a house, our character is hard to remodel. A damaged character is hard to restore and repair. Often one's character is the final item of evaluation to determine one's worthiness for a position, employment, and relationship. More than not, people's perceptions of who we are tend to be more important than what we do.

The San Diego Chargers had the first pick in the 2001 draft, but they traded their No.1 selection to the Atlanta Falcons. After visiting the Chargers, Michael Vick thought things had gone well. However, he later learned the Chargers were uncomfortable with him because of the friends he brought with him to his try-outs. To the Chargers, and despite his amazing talents, Michael Vick was thought to be too great of a risk for the Chargers to take as their top pick. The Chargers automatically assumed Vick's friends were not the right people to have around because of the image and persona they projected.[14] The character projected by his friends caused Michael Vick to be rejected despite his talents.

We all must give special effort to protect our character from the destructive nature of giants. Therefore, let us try to glean some lessons from the story of David and Goliath to help us in our constant effort to protect ourselves from giants.

Let us begin by considering what David's eldest brother said when David came down to the battlefield to ask questions about Goliath. In response to David's questions, his eldest brother said to him: *"I know thy pride."*

These words give us some indication of the importance of David's self-worth. This was a driving force which enabled David to face Goliath. The word pride means self-importance. According to his brother, David had a good sense of self-worth. David thought too much of himself to allow his character to be harmed and devastated by Goliath.

Let us apply David's self-worth to the giants of our day. For instance:

- David thought too much of himself to allow his mind and body to be destroyed by illegal drugs.
- David thought too much of his personhood to allow his identity to be defined by a gang.
- David thought too much of his dignity to wear his pants below his waist exposing himself in a disrespectful way.
- David thought too much of his ability to allow derogatory statements to be made that would reflect negatively on his capabilities.

Yes, David used a sling and a smooth stone to defeat Goliath, but it was David's good sense of self-worth that inspired him and gave him the audacity to do it.

Dr. James Harris in his book *Pastoral Theology* says how one thinks of oneself will determine, to some extent, the experiences one will pursue or not pursue for oneself. How we perceive ourselves reflects how we value our own self-worth. Therefore, what we allow to be done to us to a large extent is based upon how we view ourselves. Thus, a positive development of our self-worth is extremely important.

Laura Hillenbrand said: *"... a sense of self-worth, the innermost armament of the soul, lies at the hearts of humanness; to be deprived of it is to be dehumanized, to be cleaved from, and cast below mankind."*[15] From Hillenbrand's perspective, we can conclude that David's sense of self-worth would not allow Goliath to dehumanize him and cast him below mankind.

Ayaan Hirsi Ali in her book, *Infidel*, shares how at the age of five she could count her forefathers back for three hundred years. In my estimation that is impressive; however, she wrote that her grandmother challenged her to learn her father's ancestry eight hundred years because *"...[the] names will make you strong. They are your bloodline. If you honor them, they will keep you alive. If you dishonor them, you will be forsaken. You will be nothing. You will lead a wretched life and die alone."*[16]

Now if it is important to know the names of our ancestors to make us strong, then how far back should we go? Well, in Luke 3:23-38 (KJV), Joseph's ancestry is traced all the way back to God. Therefore, to get a proper sense of our self-worth, we need to go all the way back to God's declaration in the creation of humankind which was on the sixth day of creation. After God had evaluated all the work He had done, He declared on the sixth day of creation that it was very good (Genesis 1:31 (KJV)). So, God's declaration of our worth as human beings was very good.

Without question, a proper understanding of our self-worth begins with knowing God's declaration of who we are. When I was growing up, adults would say to me, *"You need to do this, that, and the other so that you can grow up and be somebody."* Although that is true, a greater truth is that when God made me, I was already somebody. When I was born into the world, in the words of Psalm 139:14 (KJV), *"... I am fearfully and wonderfully made: marvelous are thy works; and that my soul knoweth right well."*

I am somebody because God has said I am somebody. I do not do things to become somebody. I do things because I am somebody.

Therefore, I will not allow a giant to defy me because of who I am. I am somebody!

In reviewing David's dialog with King Saul to fight Goliath, David's sense of self-worth was all based on his relationship with God. He was able to confront Goliath because he came before him in the name of the Lord. He did not regard the battle as his own; but he recognized the battle to be the Lord's. All that David did was based on how he viewed himself in relation to God. David's relationship with God fostered his self-respect, temperance, and a positive sense of self-worth.

When we begin to understand who we are, based upon our relationship with God, our attitudes toward ourselves become affirming. In addition to that, we extend our reach beyond what is reachable to us because we personally realize that *"I can do all things through Christ which strengtheneth me."* (Philippians 4:13, KJV).

Certain things we will not allow to be done to our bodies because we understand who we are. We know that we are members of a royal priesthood. We know that we are a peculiar people. We know we are the beloved of God. We know we are the apple of God's eye. Moreover, we regard our bodies as the temples of the Holy Spirit and the Spirit of God dwells and abides in us.

David's real armament against Goliath was not his sling and the five smooth stones, but his good sense of self-worth. As a matter of fact, David only used one stone.

But why was a good sense of self-worth beneficial to David in his battle against Goliath? How did it benefit him in his fight against this giant? Well, I have identified at least four benefits that were direct results of David's good-self-worth.

First, David's good sense of self-worth gave him a great sense of pride. Right away, I know some are thinking that the Bible says in Proverbs 16:18 (KJV) that pride goes before destruction, and a haughty spirit before a fall. Yes, it does; but the word pride in the Hebrew in this verse means *to exalt oneself, to place oneself on a pedestal.* But I am referring to pride in the sense of one's own proper dignity, value, or self-respect.

Pride is a powerful character trait. It determines how we present ourselves and the care we give towards the things we do. I grew up with people constantly saying to me, *"Boy, put some pride behind the things that you do."*

In following the story of David closely, we learn about David's responsibility before we learn his name. When David is first introduced, he is introduced to us via his father in this manner, *"the youngest remains, Behold he keepth the sheep."* Following what the Bible says of David's interaction with the sheep, we discover David gave special care to the sheep he was responsible for. When David was sent to carry a half-bushel of roasted grain and ten loaves of bread to his brothers by his father, David left the sheep with a keeper. He did not leave his responsibility unguarded. That is pride.

The degree a person gives to his or her responsibility is an indication of the nature of that person's pride. The way we do things is a reflection to others of who we are. If we have a good sense of self-worth, a good perception of who we are, and a good sense of self-appreciation, then the things we do will reflect the value we have of ourselves as well as the value we wish others to have of us.

Let us always be mindful of the fact that people will label us based upon their perception of how we present ourselves. Good pride will not allow us to have certain negative connotations associated with our names. Because we are children of God, there are certain things we cannot allow to be associated with our names.

Rev. Dr. Marcus Ingram (the first African-American to get a Ph.D. in marketing at the University of North Carolina in Chapel Hill) told me that his mother once said to him, *"Boy, you may have on patches, but those patches can be clean."* That is pride. A good sense of self-worth will give us a sense of pride – good pride.

Second, David's good sense of self-worth enabled him to be tenacious. The final decision on who would fight Goliath rested with King Saul. No one could casually walk up and speak to the king. Nevertheless, David's opportunity to speak to Saul about the possibility of fighting Goliath was the result of more than one person having spoken to Saul about David.

When David heard Goliath's challenge, David began to ask what would be done for the man that killed Goliath. David's eldest brother overheard him and began to criticize David. It does not seem logical, but a proper response to criticism comes with having a good sense of self-worth.

David's brother said to him, *"Why camest thou down hither? and with whom has thou left those few sheep in the wilderness? I know thou pride and the naughtiness of thine heart"* (I Samuel 17:28, KJV).

Despite the criticism of David's eldest brother, it did not stop David. He simply responded to his brother and continued to ask questions. The scripture says that when the words were heard which David spoke, they rehearsed them before Saul: and he sent for David (I Samuel 17:31, KJV).

A good sense of self-worth will not allow others to define who we are and what we can do, but it allows us to be tenacious. It allows us to be persistent.

David would not allow his oldest brother to determine what he could or could not do. People with a poor sense of self-worth are not tenacious. They allow others to define what they can or cannot do. David's possession of good self-worth made him tenacious. Therefore, when David spoke, the people who heard him were so impressed that they went and repeated what he said to Saul.

It is a fact that we never know who is listening and watching us. The discovery of many talented people has often occurred when they were not aware that they were being watched.

We who are the children of God are supposed to be tenacious. We are supposed to be able to say to the mountain, *"move"*; and it will get out of our way. We are supposed to walk by faith declaring to others and to ourselves: *I can do all things through Christ which gives me the strength*. By our walk, we proclaim to others and to ourselves: *When I am weak, then I am strong because the power of Christ rests on me.*

Certainly, Jesus was tenacious because He always spoke as one with authority. It was said of Him that *"...never man spake like this man."*

Demons cried out when He spoke. The disciples said of Jesus, *"what kind of man is this that even the wind obeys him."* Truly Jesus exemplified the type of a tenacious spirit we should seek to possess that was driven by a sense of self-worth derived from knowing He was the Son of God. A good sense of self-worth helps us to be tenacious. If God says we can do something, then rest assured we can do whatsoever God says.

Third, David's good sense of self-worth gave him unbelievable confidence. It is unfortunate when we have abilities to do something that we allow doubt to overshadow our abilities. It is not good when others can see our abilities while we are not internally convinced of our own abilities. It takes a good sense of self-worth to have confidence.

Sometimes confidence and arrogance appear to be the same on the surface. The difference between them is what lies beneath the surface. Beneath the surface of arrogance is a haughty spirit. Beneath the surface of confidence is faith in God.

The three Hebrew boys said to King Nebuchadnezzar, *"O Nebuchadnezzar, we are not careful to answer thee in this matter. If it be so, our God whom we serve is able to deliver us from the burning fiery furnace, and he will deliver us out of thine hand, O king"* (Daniel 3:16b-17, KJV). Now, that is confidence! And Hebrews 10:35 (KJV) says *"Cast not away therefore your confidence, which hath great recompence of reward."*

By trusting God, David gained incredible confidence. This comes out clearly in David's conversation with Saul. When David initially told Saul that he would go and fight Goliath, Saul said to David: *"Thou art not able to go against this Philistine to fight with him: for thou art but a youth, and he is a man of war from his youth."* But David did not allow Saul's observation to discourage him. Instead, David conveyed to Saul how the confidence that he had in himself was based upon his faith in God. The source of David's confidence was not in himself, but in God. David said to Saul:

> [34] .... *Thy servant kept his father's sheep, and there came a lion, and a bear, and took a lamb out of the flock:* [35] *And I went out after him, and smote him, and delivered it out of*

his mouth: and when he arose against me, I caught him by
his beard, and smote him, and slew him. ³⁶ Thy servant slew
both the lion and the bear: and this uncircumcised Philistine
shall be as one of them, seeing he hath defied the armies of
*the living God ... ³⁷ moreover, The L*ORD *that delivered me*
out of the paw of the lion, and the paw of the bear, he will
deliver me out of the hand of this Philistine ... (I Samuel
17:34-37a, KJV).

David's confidence was so overwhelming and convincing until
Saul said to David, *"Go, and the L*ORD *be with thee." (I Samuel 17:37b, KJV)*

David was able to fight Goliath because he believed with God's
help he could win. David's confidence in God was so convincing until
it raised King Saul's confidence in God. Note that King Saul's final
words to David were, *"and the L*ORD *be with thee."*

A good sense of self-worth allows us to believe God can do amazing
things through our lives. It gives us confidence to confront whatsoever
we must face believing God who is with us is greater than all. To make
it in this world, we must have confidence. The basis of our confidence
must rest in what God can do through us. With God all things are
possible. A good sense of self-worth helps us to have confidence in God.

Fourth, a good sense of self-worth controls our minds and tongues.
Let us remember that a good sense of self-worth does not prevent us
from listening to the advice and the opinion of others. Let us always
be ready to listen.

After Saul agreed to allow David to fight Goliath, Saul gave David
his armor to wear. David respectfully listened to Saul's advice. David
tried what Saul suggested, but when David discovered that he could
not use Saul's armor, he took it off. David did not wear the armor
simply because Saul told him; rather, David used his own mind to
make his final decision.

It is imperative that we give attention to the advice of others. But
a sense of self-worth requires that we also must have control of our

lives. We must use our minds to make the final decisions. We must be mindful to be wise if we wish to enhance the quality of our lives.

Yes, David tried Saul's armor, but when David discovered that Saul's armor was not good for him, he stripped himself of it. With a good sense of self-worth, we listen to others but we do not allow others to think for us. David paid close attention to what he was doing. When we realize something does not fit us, or does not coincide with who we are, or does not correspond with our values, then we must yield to our good sense of self-worth which empowers us to say no. We cannot engage in things that do not correspond with our character.

Young people, you are gifted and beautiful. You are the sons and daughters of kings and queens. Yet, you must understand that a good sense of self-worth is extremely important and brings exceedingly great benefits.

Remember David! His good sense of self-worth gave him pride. It made him tenacious. It gave him confidence. It enabled him to be in control of his own mind. Above all these things, David's good sense of self-worth enabled him to be victorious over Goliath.

Always remember, we define our sense of self-worth by our relationship to the Lord Jesus Christ. In Him we are always victorious.

A praise song we sing says: "... *In the name of Jesus, the precious name of Jesus, we have the victory ... In the name of Jesus, Satan has to flee.*" No one can stand before us when we call on the great name of Jesus! In Jesus, precious Jesus, we have victory.

When we think about a good sense of self-worth, let us remember that it encourages others to invest in us.

Above all, God values us and has invested in our worth. This we know to be true because God saw so much of Himself in us that He was willing to offer up His Son (Jesus Christ) as a sacrifice to save us. Therefore, in Christ, we have the truest reality of a good sense of self-worth. Only in Him can old things be cast away; and then in Him we behold all things (even us) become new!

6

THE KEY TO SUCCEEDING: BELIEVING IN YOURSELF

The pressure to succeed rests upon the shoulders of our youth. In some respects, this begins the day they come into the world. In this sermon, Dr. Thomas describes the key to success as the art of believing in yourself.

Text: Daniel 1:18-21 (KJV)

¹⁸ Now at the end of the days that the king had said he should bring them in, then the prince of the eunuchs brought them in before Nebuchadnezzar.

¹⁹ And the king communed with them; and among them all was found none like Daniel, Hananiah, Mishael, and Azariah: therefore stood they before the king.

²⁰ And in all matters of wisdom and understanding, that the king enquired of them, he found them ten times better than all of the magicians *and* astrologers that *were* in all his realm.

²¹ And Daniel continued *even* unto the first year of king Cyrus.

To grow up in America is to be immediately met with the pressure of trying to succeed. Not long after we depart from the comforts of our mothers' wombs, and before we are even brought home from the hospital, people are wondering, what are we going to be when we grow up. Therefore, from birth, pressure is placed upon us to succeed and to be what others think we should become.

It is almost impossible to grow up in America and never feel the pressure to succeed. That is probably one of the reasons we have books such as *The Twelve Universal Laws of Success* and, *Achieving Success with Integrity.*

Needless to say, success can be a bag of mysteries. Perhaps the most prevalent mystery is understanding what it takes to succeed. That is why I sought to understand what it takes for our youth to succeed in school and in life.

I am a diligent reader of biographies and autobiographies. I believe in seeking advice and in learning from those who have been successful in things which are not well known to me. It is for that reason I have embraced the story of four teenage Hebrew boys in the Book of Daniel. These four young boys achieved success in a foreign land and their story can help us to learn what it takes to succeed.

In looking at their story, I discovered that the key to success is not complicated. It is really simple! To explain what I discovered, I need to briefly share the story of the four Hebrew boys in the Book of Daniel.

It is remarkable how these Hebrew boys were able to succeed at an extremely high level in an extremely challenging environment that was strangely different from their customs. They were originally from Jerusalem but had been brought to Babylon by the orders of King Nebuchadnezzar to be trained for special service in the king's palace. Consequently, they were removed from their family and friends. They were placed with a group of young native Babylonians with whom they had no acquaintance. In addition, their names were changed to disregard their heritage and ethnicity. They even had to learn a new language which was the language of the Chaldeans.

For three years, the four Hebrew boys were forced to live in a culture in which they were not socially entrenched. We do not know how many native Babylonians were in this select group; however, we do know the number of Hebrew boys and their names. Their names were Daniel, Han-a-ni-ah, Mi-sha-el, and Az-a-ri-ah.

Because their names were changed, we may conclude they were considered as insignificant minorities. Nevertheless, despite their adverse challenges, when these four boys came to the end of a three-year program and were taken before King Neb-u-chad-nez-zar for examination, they were at the top of their class.

Our text in Daniel 1:18-21 (KJV) says:

> [18] Now at the end of the days that the king had said he should bring them in, then the prince of the eunuchs brought them in before Nebuchadnezzar. [19] And the king communed with them; and among them all was found none like Daniel, Hananiah, Mishael, and Azariah: therefore stood they before the king. [20] And in all matters of wisdom and understanding, that the king enquired of them, he found them ten times better than all of the magicians *and* astrologers that *were* in all his realm. [21] And Daniel continued *even* unto the first year of king Cyrus.

This story is quite amazing because these teenage boys could not initially speak the language. They were not familiar with the culture and were likely ridiculed. Nevertheless, at the time of their graduation, they were the top students in their class.

But their success did not stop with their graduation. They continued to succeed beyond their graduation even in a foreign land. Daniel became chief of the governors over all the wise men of Babylon. Han-a-ni-ah, Mi-sha-el, and Az-a-ri-ah were placed over the affairs of the province of Babylon. Moreover, Han-a-ni-ah, Mi-sha-el, and Az-a-ri-ah were given higher positions in the provinces of Babylon. Daniel became the third ruler in the kingdom of Babylon. And when Da-ri-us became king, Da-ri-us selected Daniel along with two other persons to govern those he had chosen to hold offices throughout his empire. These four teenage boys, in spite of the trying circumstances that they had to endure, were able to succeed and do extremely well in a challenging and strangely different environment. Oh, how awesome that is!

For those who desire to succeed in life, I encourage you to become familiar with the story of these four teenage Hebrew boys. Seek to understand what enabled them to succeed, especially given their undesirable circumstances and situations.

Sometimes it appears complex matters require a multiplicity of answers. However, that is not necessarily true. In September 1942, Viktor Frankl, a prominent Jewish psychiatrist, and neurologist in Vienna, was arrested and transported to a Nazi concentration camp with his wife and parents. Three years later, when his camp was liberated, most of his family including his pregnant wife had perished. Nevertheless, Frankl who was known as prisoner number 119104 survived. In his bestselling 1946 book, *Man's Search for Meaning*, which he wrote in nine days about his experiences in the camps, Frankl concluded that the difference between those who lived and those who died came down to only one thing.

After looking closer at the story of the four Hebrew boys, I conclude that success in life is based on one thing: *believing in yourself.* Yes, I understand, and acknowledge, the opinions of others can be helpful or hurtful. But ultimately, the greatest impact each of us will owe to our success, or failure, is the opinion we have of ourselves.

Proverbs 23:7a (KJV) says, *"For as he thinketh in his heart, so is he."* Therefore, I challenge you to **believe in yourself.** If you do, then you will continue to discover you can accomplish far more than you have ever dreamed or imagined.

So, let us examine "what does it mean to believe in yourself?" Let us give these words some clarity, definition, meaning, and explanation. Let us clearly understand what it means to **believe in yourself**.

Rev. Jessie Jackson has said, *"I am somebody."* Okay, that is good; but help me better understand who I am. Nancy Regan used to say, *"... just say no to drugs."* Okay, that is right; but what do I do after I say no? Nike says, *"just do it."* Okay, that sounds good; but what is it I am to do and when do I stop? Yes, I agree with the slogan, *"Black Lives Matter"*;

but when does it begin to matter and how should the significance of Black lives be manifested.

I am advocating the key to success is to **believe in yourself**. Many may even agree with me. But my challenge is to explain what it means to **believe in yourself** to give this matter soundness. Therefore, I want to share three things to help explain what it means to **believe in yourself**.

First, we must first know who we are. Are you familiar with the story of the eagle that was raised by chickens? Well, being raised by chickens, the eagle thought itself to be a chicken. However, one day, the eagle looked to the skies above and noticed a group of mighty eagles soaring. Upon seeing that, the eagle cried, *"I wish I could fly like those birds."* In response, the chickens roared with laughter, saying to the eagle, *"You are a chicken and chickens do not soar."* Sadly, through a series of dialogues with the chickens, they convinced the eagle that it could never fly. Unfortunately, the eagle stopped dreaming of being able to fly. The lessons of the story are: 1) follow your dreams; 2) do not listen to the words of others who may hold you back; and 3) know who you are.

Unlike our culture, a person in the Hebrew culture knew who he or she was by his or her name. Understand that a name in the Hebrew culture expressed essence. To know a Hebrew's name was to know that person's total character and nature. By the mere fact that Daniel, Han-a-ni-ah, Mis-sha-el, and Az-a-ri-ah names were changed, the intent was to belittle them and to make fun of them.

Daniel's name was changed to Bel-te-shaz-zar. Han-a-ni-ah named was changed to Shadrach. Mi-sha-el name was changed to Me-shach. And Az-a-ri-ah name was changed to A-bed-ne-go. Thus, they were given silly names that were the names of Babylonian gods. For instance, A-bed-ne-go referred to the Babylonian god of wisdom. Shadrach referred to the Babylonian god of the moon. They were given the names of those gods to make fun of the teenage Hebrew boys and force them to honor those gods. Therefore, when people saw Daniel, Han-a-ni-ah, Mis-sha-el, Az-a-ri-ah, they would address them in a condescending manner by calling them silly names. Perhaps, they were greeted as *"hello moon"* or *"hey wisdom"*.

If we know who we are, then it does not matter what others call us. Moreover, we do not care what others may call us since we know that what they call us does not change who we are. When we know who we are, we will never be hindered by ridicule or by those who bully us with silly or hurtful names.

The four Hebrew boys knew who they were. The name Daniel meant "God is my judge". Han-a-ni-ah meant "Yah has been gracious". Mis-sha-el meant "who is what God is". And Az-a-ri-ah meant "Yah has helped". Long before coming to Babylon, these four teenage boys knew who they were.

Jawanza Kunufu states in his book, <u>Developing Positive Self-Images & Discipline in the Black Children</u>, *"People discover who they are and what they are from the ways in which they have been treated by those who surround them in the process of growing up ... The development of self-esteem emerges from the first contact the child has with his family"*[17]

Samuel D. Proctor holds, *"Personhood is best nurtured and fostered at an early age in a family."*[18]

When Albert Einstein's father, Hermann Einstein, asked Albert Einstein's headmaster what profession Albert Einstein should adopt, the headmaster said to him, *"It does not matter; he'll never make a success of anything."*[19] It is a great thing that Albert Einstein's father did not listen to Albert Einstein's headmaster. For at the age of six, Albert Einstein began to learn the violin, and seven years later was inspired by Mozart to develop an interest in the mathematical structure of music.[20] It is not surprising that Albert Einstein's father had a better understanding of who his son was than his son's headmaster.

Of course, we know our children's initial understanding of who they are begins with their parents. *"African children were, and are, held in awe because all are believed to have a specific personhood or character conferred upon them just before their souls leave heaven to be born on earth."*

The moment a child is conceived should be held in awe because the scripture teaches in Psalm 139:14 (KJV) that we are, "fearfully and wonderfully made: marvelous are thy works; and that my soul knoweth right well."

Within the depths of our souls, we know who we are, and we know God has made us for something wonderful in His eyes. Therefore, we are encouraged to hold firmly to how God has made us. Thus, for us to truly believe in ourselves we must believe we are the marvelous and wonderful works of God. As we believe in God, then we can better believe in ourselves and know who and whose we are.

Second, we must be willing to stand alone with our convictions. Let us not assume everyone is going to automatically accept what we believe about ourselves. Therefore, as we believe in ourselves, there will be times that we have to stand alone with our convictions. This is clearly seen in the text of the story when Daniel made up his mind that he would not defile himself with food and the wine the king had provided for them.

Daniel showed that he believed in himself by his willingness to stand behind his convictions. More times than not, our convictions may require of us to stand alone. More times than not, when we stand alone, we might have to suffer a loss.

Daniel's refusal of the king's food could have easily been viewed as an insult to the king; consequently, causing Daniel to lose his life. But because Daniel believed in himself, Daniel was able to stand alone upon his conviction. As we learn to believe in ourselves, we learn to hold fast to what we believe even if it means we must be alone or chance losing something material.

Daniel said to Melzar whom the prince of the eunuchs had set over them, "[12] Prove thy servants, I beseech thee, ten days; and let them give us pulse to eat, and water to drink. [13] Then let our countenances be looked upon before thee, and the countenance of the children that eat of the portion of the king's meat: and as thou seest, deal with thy servants." (Daniel 1:12-13, KJV).

If things did not go as Daniel had attended, he was willing to suffer the consequence. To believe in ourselves means to hold firmly to what we believe even if it means to suffer a loss. That loss could mean losing out on something pleasurable, relaxing, and entertaining. It may also mean separating ourselves from others to attend to our convictions.

Let us for a moment consider the story of prominent people who sacrificed much to attend to their convictions. Dr. Benjamin Mays was the president of Morehouse University from 1940 to 1967. To get an education, Dr. Mays attended his first real school in Orangeburg, South Carolina after mid-night and cleaned out-houses while others slept. Dr. George Washington Carver created more than 300 products from the peanut and 100 uses of the sweet potato. However, he walked daily in the woods before sunrise to collect samples of whatever caught his attention. Again, referring to Albert Einstein, he owed much of his success to his ability to sit quietly and think for hours on his own.

To believe in ourselves is to have confidence in our convictions. This confidence gives us courage and discipline to do certain things alone even at the risk of suffering a loss because we realize what we gain is greater than what we may lose.

Third, we must know God is with us. This might sound contradictory to the previous point. Nevertheless, to face challenges that seem too big for us to handle, there is a need to feel and know that we do not have to face it alone.

I have noticed consistently in scripture that those who were called to face strenuous and daunting challenges, or take on responsibilities beyond their abilities, were assured the presence of God. They believed God was with them to face their challenges and to help them handle their responsibilities.

For instance, consider how God was with Joseph who became second in command in the land of Egypt. Prior to this acclaim, Joseph was sold by his brothers to a band of Ishmeelites headed to Egypt. The band of Ishmeelites sold Joseph to Potiphar, who was an officer of Pharaoh. However, the scripture says in Genesis 39:2 (KJV), "And the Lord was with Joseph, and he was a prosperous man; and he was in the house of his master the Egyptian."

On the other hand, consider how God was with Moses. When God told Moses that He was going to send him to Pharaoh to bring the children of Israel out of Egypt, Moses was probably terrified because he knew the danger of challenging Pharaoh. So, Moses said unto God, *"Who am I, that I should go unto Pharaoh, and that I should bring forth the children of Israel out of Egypt?"* (Exodus 3:11, KJV). In response to the question, God said to Moses, *"Certainly I will be with thee; and this shall be a token unto thee, that I have sent thee: When thou hast brought forth the people out of Egypt, ye shall serve God upon this mountain"* (Exodus 3:12, KJV).

Another case in point is Joshua who became Moses's predecessor. After the death of Moses, Joshua was given the responsibility to continue to lead the children of Israel into the Promised Land. God said to Joshua, *"There shall not any man be able to stand before thee all the days of thy life: as I was with Moses, so shall I be with thee: I will not fail thee, nor forsake thee"* (Joshua 1:5, KJV).

Let us also consider David's battle against Goliath. It was not by a casual invitation that David got the opportunity to fight Goliath. David had to convince King Saul to give him the permission to fight Goliath. Although David was only a little shepherd boy with no experience as a soldier, David convinced King Saul with these words:

> [36] Thy servant slew both the lion and the bear: and this uncircumcised Philistine shall be as one of them, seeing he hath defied the armies of the living God. [37] David said moreover, The LORD that delivered me out of the paw of the lion, and out of the paw of the bear, he will deliver me out of the hand of this Philistine. And Saul said unto David, Go, and the LORD be with thee" (I Samuel 17:36-37, KJV).

Let us also recall the story of Mary, the mother of Jesus. When the angel Gabriel came to give Mary the announcement that she had been chosen to be the mother of the Messiah, the angel Gabriel in Luke 1:28 (KJV) spoke these words to Mary, *"...Hail, thou that art highly favoured, the Lord is with thee, blessed art thou among women."*

In each of these Biblical stories, it is clear God's presence provided

Joseph, Moses, David, Joshua, and Mary the help needed to face their challenges and to carry out their responsibilities. Similarly, it was God's presence that gave the four Hebrew boys success for their conquest. Observe what is spoken in Daniel 1:9, 17 (KJV) ["⁹ Now God had brought Daniel into favour and tender love with the prince of the eunuchs … ¹⁷ As for these four children, God gave them knowledge and skill in all learning and wisdom: and Daniel had understanding in all visions and dreams."]

Observe carefully that the four Hebrew boys were able to believe in themselves because they were aware of the presence of God with them.

I was always amazed at the will power of my niece Jaylin when she was a little girl. She was willing to do things beyond her ability or age as long as she knew I was with her.

My father in the process of accepting his call to the ministry had two vehicle accidents. In the second accident, the vehicle was completely destroyed; but my father escaped with no injuries. My father tells that immediately after the accident the Spirit of God said to him, *"As I was with you in those accidents, I will be with you in the ministry."* After that experience, my father accepted his call in the ministry and did some amazing things as a pastor.

The story is told that one night in a mass meeting during the Montgomery Bus Boycott, Dr. Martin Luther King Jr. seemed extremely flustered while delivering his speech. After the mass meeting, a person by the name of Mother Pollard came to Dr. King and said to him, *"I done told you we is with you all the way. But even if we ain't with you, God gonna take care of you."*²¹ And in the words of Paul Harvey, *you know the rest of the story.*

Some of the most comforting words of Scripture are found in Psalm 23:4 (KJV), which says: "Yea, though I walk through the valley of the shadow of death, I will fear no evil: for thou art with me; thy rod and thy staff they comfort me." Those words have been memorized and have brought comfort to many because they remind us of God's presence.

Knowing God is with us in times of despair gives us the assurance that everything is going to be all right. That is why it is so important for us to believe in God so that we might believe in ourselves. Knowing

God is with us gives us blessed assurance that we will succeed no matter what comes against us and no matter the outcome.

Young people, each of us can succeed if we grasp a clear understanding of what it means to believe in ourselves. Stumbling blocks will be thrown in our paths. Folks may call us various names to ridicule and bully us. People may even try to discredit us. Nevertheless, we can have success in whatever we do with the Spirit of the Lord upon us.

Many, including Satan, tried to stop Jesus from succeeding. They called Him names. They threw stumbling blocks in His path. They sought to discredit Him. But they could not stop him. Jesus was able to succeed because He knew the Spirit of the Lord was upon Him. He knew God (His Father) was with him. He knew God's hands were upon him. For He declares in Luke 4:18-19, "THE SPIRIT OF THE LORD IS UPON ME, BECAUSE HE HATH ANOINTED ME TO PREACH THE GOSPEL TO THE POOR; HE HATH SENT ME TO HEAL THE BROKENHEARTED, TO PREACH DELIVERANCE TO THE CAPTIVES, AND RECOVERING OF SIGHT TO THE BLIND, TO SET AT LIBERTY THEM THAT ARE BRUISED. TO PREACH THE ACCEPTABLE YEAR OF THE LORD."

7

LEARNING TO MOVE BEYOND AN ENCOUNTER WITH DISAPPOINTMENT

There are many different encounters we are prone to have in life. Unfortunately, we are bound to encounter disappointments. Since disappointments are certain, it is necessary to know how to respond. The proper response will help us to move forward with our ambitions and goals. It is for this reason that Dr. Thomas in this sermon illustrates how to respond to an encounter with disappointment. It is important, as Dr. Thomas emphasizes, to know how to respond to an encounter with disappointment. The proper response will help shape lasting virtues.

Text: Exodus 15:22-27 (KJV)

²² So Moses brought Israel from the Red sea, and they went out into the wilderness of Shur, and they went three days in the wilderness, and found no water.

²³ And when they came to Marah, they could not drink of the waters of Marah, for they *were* bitter: therefore the name of it was called Marah.

²⁴ And the people murmured against Moses, saying. What shall we drink?

²⁵ And he cried unto the LORD; and the LORD shewed him a tree, *which* when he had cast into the waters, the waters were made sweet: there he made for them a statute and an ordinance, and there he proved them.

²⁶ And said, If thou wilt diligently hearken to the voice of the LORD thy God, and wilt do that which is right in his sight, and wilt give ear to

his commandments, and keep all his statues, I will put none of these diseases upon thee, which I have brought upon the Egyptians: for I *am* the Lord that healeth thee.

27 And they came to Elim, where *were* twelve wells of water, and threescore and ten palm trees: and they encamped there by the waters.

One thing that I would suggest to our young people that I believe will be helpful to them is to read the autobiography or biography of successful people. That same suggestion was made to me in 1985 by my New Testament Professor – Dr. James Z. Alexander. Today, I am extremely grateful to him for having made that suggestion to me. To my amazement, reading autobiographies and biographies has shown me that all successful people, despite their differences, basically have an ability to overcome encounters with disappointments.

It seems that all successful people had to overcome an encounter with disappointment. For instance, consider Michael Jordan, Booker T. Washington, and Abraham Lincoln. They were all extremely successful in their endeavors at different periods of time. Yet, each of them had to overcome an encounter with one or more disappointments before they became successful. For example, Michael Jordan, who won six NBA Championships with the Chicago Bulls, failed to make the junior varsity team in the 9th grade.

When Booker T. Washington, the first president of Tuskegee University, was nearing the end of his tenure at Tuskegee University in the early 1900s, the estimated value of the school was $1,700,000 with 1,400 students, and two hundred horses. However, when Dr. Washington came to Tuskegee, he states the following in his book *Up from Slavery*: *"Before going to Tuskegee I had expected to find there a building and all the necessary apparatus ready for me to begin teaching. To my disappointment, I found nothing of the kind."*[22] When the doors were initially opened at Tuskegee University, on July 4, 1881, Dr. Washington worked from a little shanty and the use of Washington Chapel A.M.E. Church in Tuskegee, Alabama. Three months later after the opening of the school, an abandoned old plantation was purchased that came with a stable and a henhouse. That stable and henhouse were turned into a recitation room and classrooms. Then a citizen of Tuskegee gave Dr. Washington a blind horse to use on that plantation.

President Abraham Lincoln also had numerous encounters with disappointments, but he learned the importance of staying the course despite the disappointments. Before becoming the 16th President of the United States, Abraham Lincoln:

- failed in business in 1831,
- was defeated for the legislature in 1831,
- failed again in business in 1832,
- was defeated for Congress in 1843,
- was defeated again for Congress in 1848,
- was defeated for the Senate in 1855,
- was defeated for the Vice-President in 1856,
- and was defeated for the Senate again in 1858.

Moreover, as a boy, Abraham Lincoln shared a one-room log cabin with seven other people.[23] But despite all those defeats and disadvantages, Abraham Lincoln in 1860 became the 16th President of the United States.

Thus, we see that Michael Jordan, Booker T. Washington, and President Abraham Lincoln, are just a few from different eras and different careers who overcame disappointments to reach success. They all had to learn how to move beyond many disappointments to reach their goals.

Of course, I am aware that sometimes people get tired of hearing the same things said to them all the time. Young people perhaps get tired of hearing what they must do to be successful in life. I asked my nephew when he became a freshman at Toledo University (in 2012) what he liked about being in college. His response to me was, *"my freedom."* So, I understand how young people may feel. Yet, one of the most important things which those who are ambitious must learn is how to move beyond disappointments.

I know my life experiences do not capture the experiences of all. Despite that, my experiences have taught me that life is not always going to turn out the way we planned, hoped, or wished for it to be. There will be times when you will expect certain things to be and those things will not be as you expected them to be. There will also be times you will encounter things you did not expect.

I am sure many are familiar with the classic movie, The Wizard of Oz. The movie character named Dorothy discovered many things she did not expect on the Yellow Brick Road on her journey to see the

Wizard. She did not expect to encounter a lion with no courage, a scarecrow that did not have the capacity to frighten anyone, and a tin man who needed a heart.

Unexpected things in life simply happen. Who would expect during a wedding ceremony that a brother of the bride would collapse at the altar? However, that happened at a wedding I officiated on the campus of Michigan State University on July 27, 2008. In preparing for the wedding, no one expected there was a need to prepare for the bride's brother collapsing at the altar during the ceremony. Nevertheless, we responded to the brother's collapsing and continued with the wedding.

Believe it or not, that is just the way life is sometimes. Disappointing things may come upon us unexpectedly. Nevertheless, we must learn to move beyond them.

There are many reasons we must learn to move beyond disappointments. One reason might be that disappointments are not our final appointments. For God's people, our disappointments are only part of His divine plan. They may serve as a bridge to something better.

As shown in the text, there can be something good and wonderful just beyond our disappointments. Things could be developing for us that are better than we could have ever anticipated. To reach this point, it is necessary that we become driven to move beyond our encounters with disappointments. Our text provides us a perfect illustration of how this can be done. Therefore, let us take a closer look at the text.

Perhaps some are unfamiliar with the story of the children of Israel being in bondage in the land of Egypt and their deliverance from slavery in the land of Egypt. Therefore, what follows is a very brief account of the events that happened prior to the text of this message.

After a series of plagues, Moses had successfully led the children of Israel out of bondage in Egypt. Moses was an adopted child of the daughter of Pharaoh, the Egyptian leader. After killing an Egyptian, Moses fled the land of Egypt. Later, God directed him to return to Egypt to lead the children of Israel out of bondage into the Promised Land.

Moses convinced Pharaoh to release the Israelites from bondage. However, Pharaoh later had a change of mind and ordered his army to go after the children of Israel and bring them back to Egypt. Pharaoh's army pursued the children of Israel unto the Red Sea where they were encamped. With nowhere to go and no weapons to fight against Pharaoh's army, God made provision for Moses and the children of Israel to cross the Red Sea on dry land. Seeing Moses and the children of Israel crossing the Red Sea caused Pharaoh's army to hotly pursue them but only to their destruction. God closed up the Red Sea and drowned Pharaoh's army.

The point in time of our text is the ending of the third day after the children of Israel had crossed the Red Sea. However, during those three days, they had not had any water.

Imagine traveling three days without water! Imagine what it must have been like to be traveling to an unknown place, not sure of where it is or what lies ahead there. Moreover, consider the fact the Israelites were traveling three days without water with their children, the elderly, and their animals. An experience such as this would bring about frustration among many even as it did among the Israelites. There is no doubt in my mind that this frustration began to creep upon them by the second day. But after three days, they were able to come upon plenty of water at a place called Marah.

When they saw the water, it is obvious that the children of Israel were overtaken with joy, and with great expectations of relief. Perhaps their minds were renewed with energy and excitement. They were perhaps celebrating with exceedingly great joy thinking they had overcome a huge obstacle. Unfortunately, there came a harsh disappointment. The water, which they were ready to use for refreshment and to quench their thirst, turned out to be bitter.

Sadly, to say but often our excitement, elation and enthusiasm which took long to obtain can be quickly dispelled. President Nelson Mandela said, *"An advancement might take years to win, and then be rescinded in a day."*[24]

An applicable example of that is what happened to Josef and Theresa Binder of Ulm, West Germany. They became so overly filled with joy when they learned early on that Theresa was carrying twins. Theresa "thanked God for his wonderful double gift.... [This] couple bought identical baby clothes, a double cradle, and a double baby carriage as they awaited the twins' arrival."[25] But all of their joy suddenly changed when they discovered that the twin babies she was carrying were Siamese twins, joined at the back of their heads. Theresa almost lost it. She wanted to commit suicide. She even cried to God saying, "*...this can't be true! I'm not having twins! I'm having a sick, ugly monster.*"[26] This is just another example of how our joy and excitement can quickly turn to bitter sorrow.

I cannot even begin to utilize my spiritual imagination to envision how disappointing it was for the children of Israel to come upon so much water only to discover that not one drop of it could be used. They had gone three days without being able to find any water. And now the water that they found turned out to be bitter. Oh, how disappointing that must have been! It had to have been extremely disappointing to need water and to have plenty of water but not be able to use it.

We must always remember that we are not necessarily responsible for the nature of things we encounter. But with God's help, we can face every encounter.

"The key to moving forward, even in hard times, is to let your vision for your life be guided not by what you can see, but by what you can imagine."[27]

Nevertheless, through a series of events, God made the bitter water drinkable. Upon leaving Marah towards their journey to the Promised Land, the next stopover was a place called Elm which had twelve wells of water, and seventy palm trees. There the children of Israel discovered an oasis in the middle of the wilderness.

Certainly, they never anticipated or expected to have an oasis in the wilderness. They were given a lemon, but the lemon was turned to lemonade. Thus, it is necessary that we do not forget that they would have never made it to their next stop at Elm if they had not gotten beyond their encounter with disappointment.

We cannot allow disappointments to stop us. We never know what lies around the next corner. Therefore, let us not stop when we encounter disappointments. Rather, keep pressing onward as the answer to our dreams could be around the next corner.

I am not saying this will be the case in everyone's life. Yet, the truth of the matter is, we are bound to encounter disappointments in life, and we do not want to miss out on experiencing something wonderfully glorious in life because of not being able to move beyond an encounter with a moment of disappointment.

Jackie Joyner-Kersey, who won a gold medal in both the heptathlon and the long jump at the 1988 Olympics in Seoul, South Korea, believed it took that narrow defeat at the 1984 Olympics to prepare her to win two gold medals at the 1988 Olympics.[28]

Young people, those who are on the move towards something fabulous will likely face an encounter with disappointments. Yet to prove themselves to be ambitious and determined, they must gather themselves and be self-motivated to keep moving.

F. Washington Jarvis asserts that: *"It may well be that the most valuable experiences we have in adolescence are not out of triumph or our success or our popularity, but rather our disappointments and defeats and rejections. We grow more through our sufferings than through our success."*[29]

As it was with Michael Jordan, Dr. Booker T. Washington, President Abraham Lincoln, and with the children of Israel in our text, so shall it be with us. We will soon behold that there are things great and wonderful which are closer to us than we think. But to realize them, we must move beyond our encounters with disappointments.

How do we move beyond our encounters with disappointments? In other words, what do we need to understand to be able to move beyond such adversities? Let us consider four things to help us become victorious against disappointments as opposed to being defeated by them.

First, disappointments teach us things we may not know about ourselves. There are certain things we will never know until we come face-to-face with certain things. For example:

- We will never know how tall we really are until we measure ourselves.
- We will never know how we really look until we see ourselves in a mirror.
- We will never know how much we weigh until we get on a scale.

- We will never know how limited we are to what we know and how much more we can learn until we expand the boundaries of things we have been exposed to.
- We will never know what another person is genuinely like until we take the time to spend some time alone with that person.

Again let us consider Jackie Joyner-Kersey. She was raised in East St. Louis, Missouri in an environment she did not think was so bad until she left it. After leaving, her eyes were opened to other things. Leaving enabled her to realize that, she was lucky to have made it out of there.

President Nelson Mandela tells the story in his autobiography about a case that he had in a place known as *The Little Drop of Villiers in the Orange Free State.* The place was several hours from where Mandela lived in Johannesburg. President Mandela wrote: *"I am an early riser anyway, and at 3:00 a.m. the roads are empty and quiet, and one can be alone with one's thought. I like to see the coming of dawn, the change between day and night, which is always majestic."*[30] As simple as that is, it was only in leaving at a certain time in the morning that Mandela had the experience of seeing the coming of the dawn and the change between day and night. But beyond those things, this allowed him the opportunity to become acquainted with his own thoughts. Some things we will never know until we encounter certain things.

Believe it or not, it is through our encounters with disappointments that we begin to learn certain things about ourselves. Through our encounters with disappointments, we discover things missing in our lives that we need to gain and value.

In this story about the children of Israel, it is worth noting that when they discovered the water was bitter, they lost their composure and began complaining against Moses. On the other hand, and even though Moses was in the same situation with them, he began to cry out unto the Lord.

We all can be faced with similar disappointments and have different reactions. As the saying goes, *"some people see the glass as half empty while others see it as half full."* Some people say: *"let's quit; let's pack our bags, let's turn around and go home."* On the other hand, there are others who say, "we can do it; we just need to re-group and work a little harder." Observe carefully that the children of Israel complained, but Moses cried out unto the Lord.

We must understand our encounters with disappointments may cause us to know something about ourselves that we may not have known. Most importantly, it might reveal something about our attitude that reflects the level of our faith in God. Perhaps this is the difference between the children of Israel complaining while Moses cried out unto the Lord.

Perhaps our encounters with disappointments are teaching us to learn to trust God. Or maybe they are re-emphasizing we already have what we need to overcome them, and we simply need to use and lean upon what we already have. Time and time again on their journey to the Promised Land, Moses will cry out unto the Lord for help. Therefore, let our encounters with disappointments teach us more and more how to seek the Lord to help us.

Second, disappointments teach us to seek the Lord and be attentive to His directions. Those who have had encounters with disappointments know that there is a moment of not knowing what to do. We begin to feel unsure and uncertain about our predicament. Subsequently, we come to the point of not knowing what to do. Therefore, in times of uncertainty and confusion, there is only one remedy. That remedy is to seek someone who can give us directions and to attend upon the guidance, counsel, and directions we are given.

When Moses discovered the water was bitter, he cried unto the Lord. In other words, he sought God for direction. He had no other solution. He had no other one He could call upon who was able to help him in the wilderness with his problem and with the people. For help, Moses sought the Lord for direction.

Certainly, in times of confusion and uncertainty, we can perhaps seek directions from a host of people. This is fine and good. Nevertheless, we must be mindful to seek first the help of God. We should pray to God for direction because God can open our eyes to things we have not conceived. He can bring about a change in our situation with things at hand. What Moses needed to change the situation at Marah was right before him. Nevertheless, God had to show it to him. Therefore, after crying out, God showed Moses a tree to cast into the water to make the waters sweet.

Sometimes, what God will use to help us may seem unreasonable to us. But when we seek God for directions, we also must be attentive to His word and follow His directions regardless of our understanding of things. God is instructing us, and He is never wrong. God is helping us, and He will never leave us helpless or in despair.

We often seek direction from others because we believe they know things we do not know. Moses never traveled through the wilderness before, but God created and established the wilderness. Therefore, God understood things about the wilderness Moses did not know. Let us be encouraged to seek God for direction in our quest to move beyond our encounters with disappointments.

Third, when facing disappointments, we cannot be idle; but we must go to work. In the third week of March 2008, I had a situation that I will never forget. I had to be in Columbus, Ohio to preach on Sunday morning and do revival Monday through Wednesday. I was expecting to be relaxing in my hotel room around 4:00 pm on Saturday afternoon. But unexpectedly, I had an encounter with disappointment.

When I arrived in Philadelphia for my connecting flight, my connecting flight to Columbus, Ohio was canceled due to a tremendous snowstorm. I was first told I could reschedule my flight to arrive in Columbus, Ohio around 10:00 pm on Sunday. Fortunately, I was able to reach Columbus, Ohio by 1:00 am on Sunday morning.

After being told it would be Sunday night around 10:00 pm before I would arrive in Columbus, I had to go to work to arrive in Columbus around 1:00 am on Sunday morning. I had to stand in the customer service line for more than two hours. Then I had to stand in another line for another thirty minutes. I was given the last seat on a flight headed to Cincinnati. Once landing in Cincinnati, I took a taxi from Cincinnati to Columbus. The taxi ride from Cincinnati to Columbus took nearly three hours due to the snow. Nevertheless, despite a canceled flight, I still made it to Columbus, Ohio in time to preach Sunday morning. But to get there, I had to go to work.

Dr. Joel Gregory in his book, *Come Home Again – Starting over with God*, tells the story of a migrant worker from Texas named Amando Munoz who was picking tomatoes in Lake Worth, Florida when Immigration Officials swooped down demanding his papers. Munoz had lost his wallet and he could not prove that he was a U.S. citizen. Consequently, he was taken back to Mexico causing him to be twelve thousand miles from his family and home in Texas with only ten dollars in his pocket. Believe it or not, Munoz walked from where he was to Mexico City where he nearly froze at night and then he walked another six hundred miles across the country, and finally two months later; he reached a place called Matamoras. It was there that he called his 53 years old mother to tell her that he was coming home. But before Munoz could make the call, he had to go to work.

God gave Moses direction on how the water could become drinkable. For such a change to occur, Moses had to go to work. God showed Moses the tree to put in the water. Yet, Moses had to get the tree in the water. To get the tree in the water, Moses had to go to work. To move beyond an encounter with disappointment, we must be willing to go to work.

One of the things that might be overlooked in the miracles in the gospels performed by Jesus is the work the people had to do for the miracles to occur.

- Jesus turned the water into wine, but the servant had to work to bring Jesus the water.
- Jesus healed the centurion soldier's servant, but the centurion soldier had to work to find Jesus.
- Jesus healed the woman who had an issue of blood for twelve years even though she had to work to push her way through the crowd to get to Jesus.
- Jesus called Lazarus from the grave while the people had to go to work and remove the stone.

- Jesus healed a man with palsy who was brought to Him by four unnamed men. But to get that man to Jesus, those four men had to work to carry the man to Jesus. And then upon coming to the house where Jesus was, they had to take the roof off the top of the house to lower the man to Jesus.

Let us remind ourselves that Michael Jordan, Dr. Booker T. Washington, and President Abraham Lincoln had to go to work to be enabled to move beyond their encounters with disappointments.

Young people, as students, it is imperative that you learn to get beyond your disappointments with school. You must be willing to go to work. Good grades are never gained by wanting good grades alone. Good grades are the wages of hard work and seeking help when needed.

Let us reaffirm that it is necessary that we be willing to go to work in our efforts to move beyond our encounters with disappointments.

Fourth, as we face disappointments, we must understand that sometimes disappointments are designed for God to get our attention. It is sad but true that often something has to disturb us for God to get our attention. I was speaking to a person on the phone who was serving as my first line editor of a book that was going to be published. As we were talking on the phone, all of sudden, I heard in the background this big loud scream from her three-year-old son. Instantly, upon hearing the scream, she asked him, *"What's wrong?"* His immediate response was, *"this hurts."* And then she said to him, *"Haven't I talked with you about this before?"* Experiencing the hurt caused the three-year-old to get his mother's attention.

In the movie, The Color Purple, the character Shug was at the riverboat juke-joint on a Sunday. The music at the juke-joint could be heard at the church that Sunday during the morning service. Then someone in the congregation said: *God is trying to tell you something.* They started singing the saying as a song: *God is trying to tell you something.* When Shug heard the song, she stopped what she was doing, went to the church, and started singing along with the church. But before Shug could do what she did, God had to first get her attention. In Exodus 15, verse 25b-26 (KJV), it says,

> [25] ... there he made for them a statute and an ordinance, and there he proved them, [26] And said, If thou wilt diligently hearken to the voice of the LORD thy God, and wilt do that which is right in his sight, and wilt give ear to his commandments, and keep all his statues, I will put none of these diseases upon thee, which I have brought upon the Egyptians: for I *am* the LORD that healeth thee.

It was only after God had their attention, a point in time in which they were willing to listen, did God say to them the things that would be a blessing to them.

We must understand that sometimes an encounter with disappointment is designed for God to get our attention. God is trying to tell us something that will be a blessing to our lives. Until God has our attention, we cannot receive what He has for us.

Let us not be overly surprised by our encounters with disappointments. Such may not be as bad as they seem. Many lives have been saved and tremendously blessed by encounters with disappointments. New things were opened for them. Discoveries were made by them through their encounters with disappointments.

It was through an encounter with disappointment that the children of Israel received an opportunity to experience an oasis in the wilderness of twelve wells of water and seventy palm trees. Through an encounter with disappointment, they enjoyed paradise in the desert. Can you envision an oasis in the wilderness and paradise in the desert! Yet God, and God alone, can do strange and wonderful things with our disappointments.

Perhaps each disappointment we have experienced was only God's way of getting our attention so that we might have the wonderful opportunity of meeting Him. Let none of us feel bad or feel forsaken or deserted by God when we face disappointments. Our disappointments are not always simply what they appear to be on the surface or on the outside. We must look within to see what God has purposed for us through them.

Let us learn from Jesus who is our greatest example of how to face disappointments. While He was on the cross, He felt for a moment that God had forsaken Him. For the Bible says that He cried out: "MY GOD, MY GOD, WHY HAST THOU FORSAKEN ME?" Yet, God had not totally forsaken Him. Yes, God had to remove Himself from Jesus, but it was only for just a moment. It was necessary for Jesus to endure such sufferings that God might make Him to be KING of Kings, LORD of Lords, and to release all power in heaven and earth unto Him. These things we know to be so because God raised Jesus from the dead. Therefore, we can sing: *"He is Lord; He is risen from the dead; He is Lord. Every knee shall bow and every tongue confess that Jesus Christ is Lord."*

To become Lord, Jesus had to face the greatest of all encounters with disappointments. That was to be forsaken for a moment by God His Father. But in facing the greatest of all encounters with disappointments, He now reigns triumphantly over and above all. What might God have in store for us when we take courage to endure our encounters with disappointments?

8

WHAT TO DO WHEN SEEMINGLY SUCCESSFUL STEPS LEAD TO DISAPPOINTMENTS?

Disappointments can cause one to lose hope. This is especially true when goals are eagerly pursued; and when to the best of our abilities, we have taken all the right steps to achieve our goals. When our hopes and dreams are shattered, we become a prey to despair. It is for this reason that Dr. Thomas has devoted this sermon to give us divine directions to help us deal with disappointments. Dr. Thomas strongly reminds us that disappointments prune us for great success stories.

Text: Job 31: 1-8, 35-40 (KJV)

[1] I made a covenant with mine eyes; why then should I think upon a maid?

[2] For what portion of God *is there* from above? and *what* inheritance of the Almighty from on high?

[3] *Is* not destruction to the wicked? and a strange *punishment* to the workers of iniquity?

[4] Doth not he see my ways, and count all my steps?

[5] If I have walked with vanity, or if my foot hath hasted to deceit;

[6] Let me be weighed in even balance, that God may know mine integrity.

[7] If my step hath turned out of the way, and mine heart walked after mine eyes, and if any blot hath cleaved to my hands;

[8] *Then* let me sow, and let another eat; yea, let my offspring be rooted out.

[35] Oh that one would hear me! behold, my desire *is, that* the Almighty would answer me, and *that* mine adversary had written a book.

[36] Surely I would take it upon my shoulder, *and* bind it *as* a crown to me.

[37] I would declare unto him the number of my steps; as a prince would I go near unto him.

[38] If my land cry against me, or that the furrows likewise thereof complain;

[39] If I have eaten the fruits thereof without money, or have caused the owners thereof to lose their life:

[40] Let thistles grow instead of wheat, and cockle instead of barley. The words of Job are ended.

We should not become numbed, outraged, or torn apart by an encounter with disappointment. It is a guaranteed part of life that we will experience or encounter disappointment.

I have to agree with the person who said, *"...the only person who has never experienced disappointment in life is a person who has never tried or attempted to do anything in life."*

Alexander Pope penned, *"Blessed is the man who expects nothing, for he shall never be disappointed."*

Let us understand we will experience disappointments if we have life-long dreams, goals, and aspirations. Even if we do not have such things, we will still find disappointments lurking around us to make life unpleasant for us.

Let us therefore not be ashamed when we face disappointments. Let us lift our heads because, though it might sound strange, disappointments are adventures that help make a healthy life. George Augustus Lofton said, *"He that has never stumbled nor fallen – never erred nor done wrong – has never traveled far nor attempted much."*

Certainly, it is true that disappointments take on a different light, a different nature, and a different meaning when we have followed the rules. Disappointments do not seem fair when we have done all the things we are supposed to do in the order and manner they were to be done. Such disappointments are terribly hard to reckon with and terribly hard to accept.

Consider some common analogies. For example, it is disappointing to follow a cake recipe in detail and in the end the cake flops. Another case in point is to have strictly followed directions to a certain place only to be found lost in an unknown place.

So, what should we do when we fall upon disappointments? How should we respond when we have seemingly taken all the right steps; we have done the things we were told to do; and we have walked the true paths conventionally marked for success? How do we deal with such disheartening experiences?

Well, I believe there is not a person more qualified to give advice on circumstances of that nature than the Biblical character Job. We should pay close attention to his life. The things Job experienced would

---

appear to most to be inconsistent with the pathways Job had taken for his life. Job said of himself: "My foot hath held his steps, his way have I kept, and not declined" (Job 23:11). Nevertheless, Job still experienced an unbelievable set of disappointments.

Let us remember that Job was described as a perfect and upright man. He feared God and avoided evil. God said that there was none upon the face of the earth like Job. He was a godly man, a family man, and a rich man. Despite his fame and possessions, Job lost all his children and his riches and came into a great battle with his health.

We all should read and re-read the Book of Job which has forty-two chapters. Chapters 4 through 31 record the conversations between Job and his three friends whose names were Eliphaz, Bildad, and Zophar. They came to visit Job during the time of Job's severe sickness.

The conversations between Job and his friends were their attempts to explain Job's troubles. It was a common theological and prevailing belief that a man's troubles were the results of his own sins. According to Job's friends, goodness and evil do not randomly fall upon a person. The retribution for doing something good versus doing evil was not the same.

Observe some of the things Job's friends said to him. Eliphaz said in Job 4:7 (KJV): "whoever perished, being innocent, or where were the righteous cut off?". In Job 8:3, Bildad said: "Doth God pervert judgment? or doth the Almighty pervert justice?". Zophar in Job 20:5 (KJV) said: "the trumping of the wicked is short, and the joy of the hypocrite but for a moment"

Clearly, Job's friends were thoroughly convinced Job's problems were his own misfortunes. From their perspective, Job's predicament only justified their arguments.

Despite the accusations of his friends, Job maintained his innocence. He said in Job 16:19 (KJV): "my witness is in heaven, and my record is on high. God knows the way that I take: and when he hath tried me, I shall come forth as gold." From the bottom of his heart, Job believed he had not done things to cause him to be in such great trouble. Therefore, to defend his innocence, Job retraced the steps he had taken in life.

From his perspective, Job believed his situation was inconsistent with the order of his life. In Chapter 31, Job basically says that he can accept what has happened to him if certain conditions in his life were true. In other words, he could accept and understand his situation:

- if he walked in vanity,
- if he had hasted to deceit,
- if his heart had walked after his eyes,
- if he had withheld things from the poor,
- if he had not shown concern for the fatherless,
- if he had those in need to perish for want of clothing,
- if he had made gold or money his hope and his confidence,
- if he had rejoiced because his wealth was great, or
- if he had rejoiced at the destruction of those who hated him.

Job was not guilty of these transgressions. Yet, Job still experienced a period in his life where he had seemingly unexplainable disappointments. In his last words to his friends, Job expressed his frustration over the inconsistency between what he had done in life versus what life had given back to him with these words found in Job 31:35 (KJV): "Oh that one would hear me! behold my desire *is, that* the Almighty would answer me ..."

Many of us can identify with Job's frustration. I know for myself, there have been times when I did things which I thought were right only to receive unexpected results. I followed the instructions for success that were given to me by my parents, my grandparents, my Sunday School teachers, and others. I went to school, worked hard, and took pride in being honest. I tried to carry myself in a respectful way. I did my best with whatever I was given. I went back to school, and back to school again. I did not hang out in the streets. I even avoided certain crowds and abstained from substance abuse. Despite all of that, I still landed from time to time in the way of disappointments.

It is very hurtful and deflating to follow the proper path for a successful life and find that it detours into the way of disappointments.

Such things as these break our momentum. Setbacks occur and we can easily be overtaken by grief.

Nevertheless, I can say without any hesitation or reservation that I grew during and through those disappointing times. My maturity increased and I learned more about myself and about God. Thus, I now can identify with wise words of Faye Angus who said:

> *If we lived only on the mountaintops of life, our souls would be barren. It is in the deep and low places, often the places hidden from everyone but God; it is in the valleys of sorrow and our griefs that we cultivate understanding, compassion, courage, sensitivity, sympathy, kindness and all those tender mercies. The mountaintop maybe quiet and peaceful, and even a restful place to be, but growth takes place only in the valleys.*

It is a paradox when things done properly and orderly to achieve success result in disappointments. Yes, we hurt; but we also benefit greatly. Consequently, it is important for us to understand what to do when disappointments creep upon us as we properly pursue noble endeavors. There are three things I would like to suggest we consider to help us victoriously cope with disappointment.

First, we must check our motives. Oftentimes we are disappointed when we have taken the right steps because our motives are inconsistent with our steps. Yes, we did the right things, or we took the right steps, but for the wrong reasons. Therefore, things did not turn out the way we anticipated. We must understand that God will not bypass our intentions for the sake of a successful outcome. With God, the end does not justify the means. Job said: "my heart shall not reproach *me* as long as I live." (Job 27:6, KJV) Only the pure in heart, declared Jesus, shall see God.

As Christians, our motives ought to be controlled by our values. Christian values are shaped by what we believe about God. Not success but faithfulness must be the aim of a Christian. The word success is only mentioned once in the Bible. It is found in Joshua 1:8 (KJV).

However, the emphasis there to Joshua was not what he would obtain, but what he would be. Our value system as followers of Christ is not based initially upon what we accomplish, but rather by what and who we seek to be.

Sometime ago, I watched a documentary about a man who started out as a janitor at Rosedale High School located in a small town outside of Atlanta, Georgia. This man went back to school at night, earned his degree, and eventually became the head basketball coach at the same school where he once served as janitor. He was named coach of the year several times without ever winning a state basketball championship until 1991, if my recall is correct. While looking over the transcripts of his players, the coach discovered that one player was academically ineligible. The player was one whom he had brought up from the junior varsity and had only played a total of 43 seconds throughout the entire state playoffs. The coach said many thoughts entered his mind regarding what he should do. But he remembered the things that he had taught his players. He had taught his players that there was more to life than just simply winning. The coach said that he had to uphold the things he had taught his players. Therefore, he forfeited his one state championship to demonstrate the importance of having values in everything we do. This was certainly an act of incredible integrity. There was one thing the coach said during the interview which I will always remember. The coach said that *"our religion ought to shape our values."* And for him, he emphasized that it was not so much what he accomplished but rather who he was.

As Christians, we must remember that our motives in whatever we do ought to be controlled by a desire to do God's will. Therefore, when we are disappointed after taking seemingly successful steps, we can take comfort in knowing we have tried to do God's will. What is most important is not necessarily what we accomplish but being faithful to the will of God. As it is stated in the Book of Hebrews, some of our forefathers of the faith died not having received the promise.

Second, we must look for alternatives. The old saying, *"God works in mysterious ways and has wonders to perform,"* is so true. God has a way that is not like our way. God sometimes closes doors; or He allows us to experience disappointments so that we can enter better doors.

Harry Emerson Fosdick has a sermon entitled, "Handling Life's Second-Bests." In that sermon, Fosdick said *"that very few persons have a chance to live their lives on the basis of their first choice. We all have to live upon the basis of our second and third choices."*[31] Therefore, when our first choice in life is not available to us, we must look for alternatives.

There is often some compensation in every trial if we look hard enough for it. There is also basically an alternative to everything we do. We must, however, be willing to look hard enough to find it.

Nick Vujicic was born with no arms and no legs, but he wanted to dress himself. Of course, with no arms, shirts with buttons were a great challenge for him. So, to resolve that problem his parents found shirts that he could slip on, and off, by throwing the shirts over his head and twisting his body into them.[32] Clearly, he found an alternative.

Nate King Cole was a great singer and jazz pianist, but his parents refused to buy him a piano. Therefore, he painted eighty-eight black and white keys of a piano keyboard on the windowsill to practice. Thus, he discovered an alternative for his dream.

The young surfer Bethany Hamilton lost her left arm after a shark attack. Consequently, she learned to surf with one arm to continue her quest to compete in surf competitions. In learning to surf with one arm, she said, *"I had to learn to paddle evenly with one arm, and when I felt the wave pick me up, I had to put my hand flat on the center of the deck to lift my feet rather than grabbing the surfboard rail the way you would if you had two hands."*[33] Bethany Hamilton prudently sought an alternative to achieve her ambitions.

One of the biggest misconceptions about happiness is that it is something we find. Happiness is not something that we find, but something that we create. Life is not what we find but what we create.

Consider the story of Louis Braille who became blind at the age of three due to an accident. Although he was blind, Louis wanted to continue to learn. Unfortunately, he could not learn everything by listening. Therefore, Louis developed and published the first tactile system for reading and writing for the blind. He used a pattern of six raised dots to represent letters, punctuation marks, and mathematical symbols. Louis Braille developed another way for the blind to read and write and the first Braille book was published in 1829.

Glennis Siverson is an award-winning photographer who is legally bind. Glennis said, *"Prior to losing most of my eyesight, if I was doing portrait photography, I was focused on every strand of hair and every angle of the person's body. My work looked stiff because I was so focused on composition. But now my approach is pretty much a gut reaction. I feel it; I see it; and I shoot it. My work is more instinctual."*[34] This is truly an amazing story. Since she lost much of her eyesight, Glennis has won ten international awards for her portrait and landscape photography.[35]

The Disabled Artist Association (DAA) was started by a German-born artist Arnulf Erich Stegmann in 1956. Stegmann was stricken with polio when he was three years old and lost the use of his hands and arms. He began to learn to write, holding a pencil between his teeth. Using the same method, he learned how to paint; and at an exceedingly early age he was a star pupil in the art school he attended. When he was barely twenty years old, Stegmann's work was exhibited in several countries in Europe.[36]

When Booker T. Washington went to Tuskegee, he was expecting to find a building and all the necessary apparatus ready for him to begin teaching but discovered a disappointing situation. Dr. Washington did not allow his disappointment to defeat him. On the contrary, he began to create and look for alternatives. He found an old dilapidated shanty near a black Methodist Church. From there, he opened the doors of Tuskegee Institute on July 4, 1881. Three months later, Dr. Washington purchased a farm and turned the henhouse into a classroom. A citizen of Tuskegee gave Dr. Washington a blind horse to use on the farm. The buildings were built from bricks that the students made. In the writing of his autobiography, Dr. Washington stated that he had turned what was valued as nothing into a property that had an estimated value of $1,700,000. His enrollment grew from 30 students initially to 1400 students. One blind horse turned into two hundred horses. It is not what you find in life, but what you make out of life by being creative with alternatives.

Dr. Martin Luther King Jr. made his place of incarceration in the Birmingham jail a place to write his most effective letter during the Civil Rights Movement. Malcolm X made his incarceration a place to educate himself. The Bible character named Joseph made his incarceration in Egypt an opportunity to become second in command in the land of Egypt.

When seemingly successful steps lead to disappointments, then it is necessary that we become creative and look for alternatives. We discover those alternatives by seeking the LORD through prayer and through the counsel of His Word to guide us and to help us.

Third, we must understand that it is not what we obtain that is ultimately important, but rather what we hold on to. This is where we really receive help from Job. In spite of all that Job went through, Job held to his integrity.

Regarding Job, God said to Satan, "he still holdeth fast his integrity, although thou movedst me against him, to destroy him without a cause" (Job 2:3, KJV). Job's wife asked him, "dost thou still retain thine integrity? curse God and die" (Job 2:9, KJV).

Many things were taken from Job, but what was most important to Job could never be taken away. Job could only lose it by letting it go. But Job held on to his integrity.

I was totally impressed by a story I read in the May 2012 Edition of Reader Digest. The story was about a man who found $45,000 in the attic of his new house and returned the money to its owner. Based on the way the man found the money, it justifiably belonged to him. While being in the attic, he recognized a World War II ammo box in which he discovered $800 tied up with orange twine. He also found seven other boxes and two large trash bags full of cash in them. The total amount of cash he discovered was about $45,000 (Reader Digest, May 2012, page 168). After finding the money, the man's first thought was, "this was a blessing from God." Soon thereafter he concluded the right thing to do was to return the money to the prior owners who had no idea that the money was in the attic. The following Christmas, the man used the orange twine to tie up Christmas presents as a reminder of the priceless treasures of honesty and integrity.

Our integrity must never be something that can be taken away from us. Let it never be surrendered for anything.

Tony Dungy in my estimation provides a beautiful definition of integrity. He says, *"integrity is that internal compass and rudder that directs you to where you know you should go when things around you are pulling you in a different direction."*[37]

When successful steps lead to disappointments, find great joy in knowing that you stayed the course with your internal compass and rudder.

Brand Ronnell Braxton in a sermon entitled, "The Greatest Temptation", states that *the greatest temptation is to be ordinary, or to be like everybody else.* Everyone else is doing it. Why can't we? Well, it is because we are Christians with an internal compass and rudder given us by faith in God – thus our integrity.

There is great joy in knowing we have held to the internal compass and rudder within us and have not joined the ordinary. Furthermore, when we hold onto our integrity it will be recognized. Subsequently, great admiration will come from observers and from God Himself.

Despite disappointment, Job did not join in with the ordinary. Job continued to be ethically sound and upright before God.

Our circumstances must never alter the source which defines our integrity. Therefore, our relationship with God must be the same whether we are up or down; whether we are in a storm or walking joyfully in the sun; whether we are trying to make it through the night or scrolling happily during the day; whether we are sick or well; whether our barrels are running over or at rock bottom; whether things are favorable or unfavorable.

Disappointments will attempt to snatch away our integrity. This is especially true when we have taken the right steps, followed the advice of wisdom, and done our best. Yet, we must regard our integrity and our faith as powerful sources of our inner being that we will not allow to be taken away from us. We hold these things as precious gifts of God and of greater value than any earthly pursuit or possession. Carnal things can be replaced but nothing can take the place of integrity and faith. We must never surrender these virtues for any reason or cause.

When successful steps lead to disappointments, let us remember to check our motives; let us look for alternatives in life; and let us hold to our integrity at all costs.

Our challenge as Christians is to endure. The prize is not given to the swift nor the strong, but to the one who endures to the end.

We can be encouraged to endure by many characters in the Bible and by many of our forefathers. When they were tried or when they were disappointed, they all held fast to their faith in God. They retained their integrity under great pressures and emerged heroes of faith.

Let us make our aim in life to be that we held fast to our integrity and "kept the faith". Perhaps there will be storms but let us be determined to keep the faith. No doubt, there will be false accusations made, but still be driven to keep the faith. Unfortunately, we are likely to be wounded by diverse hurts, but still let our commitment be to keep the faith. Despite being forsaken by many whom we may regard as dear and close, even so let these misfortunes not hinder us from keeping the faith. Blessings will come to those who endeavor to hold fast to their integrity by trusting God with unwavering faith.

In all things, consider Jesus. As we look at His life, we can agree that Jesus always did right. Yet, He ended up on an old rugged cross. They tried to cause Him to let go of His integrity, but He remained true to His hope in God. Because Jesus remained faithful to God, He now has been given all power to reign as the Sovereign Lord over all.

An old hymn reminds us to hold to God's unchanging hands. It further encourages us to build our hopes on things eternal. By such, we will be victorious over all our disappointments.

9

STICKING WITH IT UNTIL YOU GET IT

Unfortunately, there are times when it appears our goals are too difficult to achieve. They may even appear to be beyond our reach. During such times, we need to know how to stick with it until we get it. In this sermon, Dr. Thomas lays out some guidelines to help us accomplish our goals. That is why the title of this sermon is, Stick with It until You Get It.

Text: Luke 18:35-43 (KJV)

[35] And it came to pass, that as he was come nigh unto Jericho, a certain blind man sat by the way side begging:

[36] And hearing the multitude pass by, he asked what it meant.

[37] And they told him, that Jesus of Nazareth passeth by.

[38] And he cried, saying, Jesus, *thou* Son of David, have mercy on me.

[39] And they which went before rebuked him, that he should hold his peace: but he cried so much the more, *Thou* son of David, have mercy on me.

[40] And Jesus stood, and commanded him to be brought unto him: and when he was come near, he asked him,

[41] Saying, What wilt thou that I shall do unto thee? And he said, Lord, that I may receive my sight.

[42] And Jesus said unto him, Receive thy sight: thy faith hath saved thee.

[43] And immediately he received his sight, and followed him, glorifying God: and all the people, when they saw *it*, gave praise unto God.

The stories of people who became famous through their achievements are very encouraging to me. I am sure things for many of these people did not always go as they had planned; but they were still able to achieve. Their stories include many encounters with disappointments as they pursued their dreams. Some had setbacks when they thought that they were on the verge of moving forward. Some were discouraged and were told they would never achieve anything. Yet, despite things not always going as planned, they all never quit; and they never gave up on their dreams.

Without question, Albert Einstein was one of the greatest scientists the world has ever known. But ironically, he was considered a slow learner and retarded as a child. It is said that Einstein's father asked the school principal what profession his son should adopt. In response, the principal simply said: *"it doesn't matter; he'll never make a success of anything."*[38]

There is also the story of Byron Pitts who was a correspondent for the CBS News broadcast called 60 Minutes. Pitts was also the chief national correspondent for CBS News in January 2009. His freshman English Professor at Ohio Wesleyan University said to him: *"Mr. Pitts, you are wasting my time and the government's money. You are not Ohio Wesleyan University material. I think you should leave."*[39]

The story of Wilma Rudolph is just as intriguing. Rudolph did not begin school until she was 7 years old because she was crippled. Yet, she became the first woman to win three goal medals in the Olympics competing in track and field events in Rome in 1960.

The stories behind famous people like those I have cited are filled with encouragement and inspiration. These stories are reminders that we can achieve whatever we set out to do if we are willing to plow through the disappointments, setbacks, and the discouragements we may encounter along the way.

As we set out to accomplish our dreams and our goals, there is always the possibility that things may go wrong. A stumble and a fall are quite common incidents. We all have stumbled or stumped a toe while walking; or perhaps we have slipped on something. Any way you look at it, if there is a possibility for something to go wrong, it will.

When things go wrong, or when things do not turn out the way we planned, we should not fold up our tents and take these as signs that the time has come for us to quit. Rather, we should remember this saying: "success is going from failure to failure with no loss of enthusiasm".

"Thomas Edison, who went through more than ten thousand failed experiments before he developed a commercial light bulb, said most of those who consider themselves failures are people who did not realize how close to success they were when they gave up. They were almost there: going through failure, but still bound for success. But they gave up before the tide could turn for them."[40]

Many great discoveries have come through trial and error. Those who aspire for and achieve excellence often experience some degree of failure before they embrace success.

Alonzo Mourning was an NBA all-star seven times and was twice named NBA Defensive Player of the Year. He earned an NBA championship in 2006 with the Miami Heat. He was also a member of United States Gold Medal Basketball Team in the 2000 Olympics. Mourning said, *"...as painful as our mistakes can be, they can also turn out to be blessings. I think that is the only thing you can take from a mistake – a lesson."*[41]

It is unfortunate many people give up too soon. They throw in the towel and abandon the race before crossing the finish line. They experience a bit failure, perhaps repeatedly, and stop pursuing their goals and their dreams, not realizing the lessons they are learning along the way.

This might sound bizarre, but disappointments, setbacks, and discouragements always arise to hinder every good ambition. Therefore, it is necessary that we know how to persevere when we face such negative things that can take the wind out of our sail. It is imperative that we have what it takes to **stick with it until we get it**.

The blind man in our text knew how to persevere until he got what he wanted. He only wanted to receive his sight and he persevered through faith to receive it.

The wonderful thing about the story of the blind man is the fact that he received his sight despite being rebuked and discouraged by many. Therefore, let us try to understand what gave the blind man the boldness to not give up his quest to receive his sight.

The blind man stuck with it until he received his sight. We should carefully examine his story which includes a multitude of factors, including: aspiration, bravery, courage, determination, energy, fortitude, guts, hunger, inspiration, joy, kick, liberation, motivation, nerves, obsession, passion, qualification, resolve, stimulation, tenacity, unction, vitality, will, x-factor, yearning, and zeal.

It is evident from the conversation Jesus had with him that it was the blind man's faith that allowed him to receive his sight. He plowed through whatever stood in his way to receive his sight. When asked by Jesus what he wanted, the blind man simply said that he wanted to receive his sight. Then Jesus said to him: *"Receive thy sight: thy faith hath saved thee."*

The blind man teaches us that faith in God enables and inspires us to **stick with it until we get it**. He shows us that faith conquers disappointments, setbacks, and discouragements. By faith we become persistent in the pursuits of our goals and dreams even when things go wrong, or do not turn out the way we have planned.

The Psalmist said in Psalm 27:13 (KJV), *"I had fainted, unless I had believed to see the goodness of the* Lord *in the land of the living."*

To keep going amidst negative forces, we must have faith in God. For us to stick with something good to the end requires that we learn to place our faith in God.

Faith in God gives us the spirit of determination. The more we trust God the more we will increase in being determined to achieve our ambitions. We can easily be discouraged when things do not go the way we have planned or thought things should go. But by faith we remain focused on the power of God to help us while avoiding being distracted by negative encounters.

Let us take note of the blind's man faith to help us understand his determination to stick with it until he received his sight.

First, the blind man's faith allowed him to be prepared to take advantage of the opportunity that came his way. We learn from the text that before the blind man received his sight, he was by the roadside begging. During those days, it was typical for a blind person to make a living by begging. But when he learned that Jesus was passing by, he stopped begging and began to cry out saying: "Jesus, *thou* Son of David, have mercy on me." He recognized that an opportunity had been presented to him to receive his sight.

Jesus passing by was not a regular day for the blind man. On this day people were traveling to Jerusalem for the Passover. Perhaps the blind man considered this day as an opportunity to make a lot of money begging due to the crowds making their way up to Jerusalem. For him, it was like our Black Friday – the Friday sale after Thanksgiving – an opportunity to receive far more than usual. Some opportunities we have only come once in a lifetime. Therefore, we cannot afford to allow such opportunities to pass us by.

As the text explains, the story of the blind man took place near Jericho. Jesus, however, was not coming to Jericho to stay; rather He was only passing through on his way to Jerusalem. Since the blind man was unable to see, he had to ask the reason for the noise he was hearing. Surely, he had heard about Jesus but perhaps never thought Jesus would come his way. No doubt he thought if Jesus came near then he would ask Him for something greater than money. He would ask Him for his sight. Consequently, the blind man realized when he heard Jesus was passing by that this was perhaps a once in a life-time opportunity. Therefore, he had to seize the moment at all costs. So as the opportunity came to him, he stopped begging for money and began to cry out, "Jesus, *thou* Son of David, have mercy on me."

Of the many things to understand about faith, it is most important to understand that faith prepares us to watch for enabling opportunities that will advance our cause. There is a song which the gospel group called the Clark Sister sings which says, *"I am looking for a miracle ... I expect the impossible ... I feel the intangible ... I see the invisible."* This song reinforces our faith to always be on the alert for unseen blessings God has in store for us.

Faith is the substance of things hoped for and the evidence of things not seen. We are on the alert because we are hoping for the opportunities which are coming our way. We are expecting and looking for God to make a way, show us the way, or provide the way for us in the manner He chooses that is best for us and brings glory to Him. Job said: "all the days of my appointed time will I wait, till my change come." (Job 14:14, KJV).

It is necessary that we observe what the blind man had to do to take advantage of the opportunity before him. He had to temporally let go of his preoccupation with begging. Literally, he had to stop using his voice for begging. Instead, he used it to cry out, "Jesus, *thou* Son of David, have mercy on me."

In seizing opportunities, we must be willing to let go of certain things, especially those things that are lesser in value than the opportunity presented to us. There are some things we must lay aside right now when the opportunity for an education is given to us. An education is an imperative because it creates opportunities for us. Therefore, we must lay aside things that are of lesser value when the opportunity for education comes to us. We must put aside laziness. We must not spend too much time watching TV. Furthermore, we must use our time wisely; and not waste it talking on the phone or playing games. We must learn how to lay aside idleness for the greater good of an education and the opportunities it breeds.

We seize opportunities by faith. It is the power which gives us the ability to believe in what is better and greater. Faith enabled the blind man to cast aside his begging occupation and take advantage of the opportunity to cry out to Jesus that he might receive his sight.

Second, faith enabled this blind man to use what he had. As we understand blindness, we know the blind man could not see. He did not see Jesus passing by, but he heard the noise of the crowd, and he asked what was going on. Although this blind man did not see Jesus passing by, he used his ears and his mouth to discover Jesus was near.

One Friday, on the 13th day of September, after a meeting at the Martin Street Baptist Church in Raleigh, North Carolina; I went to a restaurant with a minister friend for lunch. As we were leaving, there was a young man at the register whose right arm was cut off.

I was fascinated by the way he counted the money in the register. Typically, we hold money in one hand and count it with the other. On the contrary, this young man held the money under the arm of his shorter right hand as he counted money. This young man did not have two normal hands, but he used what he had to get the job done. I marveled as I watch this young man use what he had to do his job.

To stick with a goal until we achieve it requires that we learn to use what we have. We cannot use what we do not have; but what we do have we can use. Whatever we need to succeed, we must know that God gave it to us when we were born. But we must use it.

Nick Vujicic says, *"...for every disability you have, you are blessed with more than enough abilities to overcome your challenges."*[42]

Miss America 1995, Heather Whitestone, was deaf. For her performance, she danced by the music of Via Dolorosa by Sandi Patti. People wondered how Whitestone heard the music. Her response was, *"I can hear some sound with my hearing aid. But what I do is feel the music and listen to the music...for a couple of time. Then I count the number with the music and memorize it in my heart. And that's how I do it."*[43].

Faith helps us to use what we have. At the Red Sea, God asked Moses: *"what do you have in your hand?"* Using what he had, God empowered Moses to open the Red Sea for the children of Israel to cross on dry land.

Faith inspires us to take what we have and use it to the best of our ability. We depend on God to bless us. We trust Him to make all things work together for our good and for His glory. By faith we can stick with our goals until we achieve them, using what we have.

Third, the blind man's faith enabled him to plow through discouragement. Perhaps one of the best African-American preachers of our time is the late Dr. A. Louis Patterson of Houston, Texas. Dr. Patterson tells the story of what his pastor said to him when he shared with his pastor his calling to the ministry. When he made the announcement to his pastor, Dr. Patterson says his pastor laughed at him. And then his pastor said to him, *"How could the Lord have called you to preach when you cannot even talk?"* At that time, Dr. Patterson had a speech impediment. He responded to his pastor by saying: *"I do not know. All, I know is that the Lord has called me to preach."*

The President of Bob Jones University told Dr. Billy Graham when he was a young preacher that he would never amount to anything. In our times, there is perhaps no preacher as well-known as Dr. Billy Graham.

Barry C. Black interviewed for the Senate chaplain's job. Unfortunately, many thought he had a better chance of winning the lottery, but he proved them wrong.

Matt Rolf designs complex computer systems in Hillsboro, Oregon. Because of his stature, his kindergarten teacher told his mother that Matt was never going to set the world on fire for he was just an average student. Unfortunately, Matt's kindergarten teacher did not see the giant inside of him.

Dr. A. Louis Patterson, Dr. Billy Graham, Dr. Barry C. Black, and Matt Rolf plowed through many types of discouragements to reach great heights in their professions.

The multitudes rebuked the blind man when he initially cried out, "Jesus, *thou* son of David, have mercy on me." But the text says that he cried so much the more. He resisted discouragement by elevating his crying out from an ordinary loud shout to attract attention (Luke 18:38, KJV) to an instinctive shout of ungovernable emotion (Luke 18:39, KJV). In other words, he screamed with the likeness of an animal cry to drown out discouragement and to get Jesus' attention. In other words, the blind man went berserk resisting the rebukes he was receiving from the multitude. He overlooked the multitude and began to scream to the top of his voice - *"Thou* son of David, have mercy on me." By faith, the blind man plowed through discouragement.

We must plow through discouragement to reach our goals. We do so by holding on to what we know the Lord has told us. We may have many reasons to be discouraged but we must encourage ourselves with the promises the Lord has given to us.

Perhaps we all remember the story of the Little Blue Engine trying to get the toys on the other side of the mountain. The Little Blue Engine kept saying to itself, *"I think I can. I think I can. I think I can. I think I can."* When the train was hitched to the Little Blue Engine, the Little Blue Engine tugged and pulled, and pulled and tugged; and then slowly the Little Blue Engine started pulling the train. While pulling the train, the Little Blue Engine started puffing and chugging, but continuously saying to itself, *"I think I can. I think I can. I think I can. I think I can."* Despite gravity pulling against it, as it was going up the side of the hill trying to reach the top of the mountain, the Little Blue Engine kept saying to itself, *"I think I can. I think I can. I think I can. I think I can."* And finally, the Little Blue Engine made it to the top of the mountain and to the other side. The moral of the story is that the Little Blue Engine made it by believing it could. Despite the load, the Little Blue Engine plowed through discouragement to reach the top of the mountain.

It takes faith in God to plow through discouragements. If God says we can do it, then it can be done. This keeps us going when discouragements come because we know we can do all things through Christ who gives us strength.

Fourth, we must know what we want. After the blind man had suffered through being rebuked and discouraged, the text says Jesus stopped. When we become serious and sincere about what we are doing, people will stop and take notice of our persistence. The blind man was relentless until Jesus sent for him. And when Jesus sent for him, Jesus asked the blind man what he wanted. The man was truly clear and precise in sharing with Jesus what he wanted. The text says he said, "Lord, that I may receive my sight."

It is unfortunate but many people fail to stick with it until they get it because they are not sure of what they want. Persistence is driven by knowing what we want and what we want to be.

Byron Pitts initially struggled with literacy and speech but he says that his inspiration to pursue journalism had deep root. Pitts asserts, *"[he] took as signs from God that communication would play a major role in [his] life."*[44] He was convinced through scripture like Romans 12:2 (KJV), "Be not overcome of evil, but overcome evil with good." He also believed that *all the bad things in life had some good purpose only if he searched long enough.*[45] Thus he concluded journalism was his purpose.[46] Byron Pitts did not allow his illiteracy and his speech impediment to stop him from pursuing what he wanted to be because he knew what he wanted to be. He also says, *"It is amazing how you can transform a dream into a reality by saying it until you believe it and others believe it with you."*[47]

But knowing what we want to do or be also includes being willing and ready to accept the responsibilities that come along with what we desire. Although there were disadvantages, there were also some advantages to the man being blind. Ironically, he could not work but he made his living by humbling himself to ask help of others. Perhaps we can say that he begged with honor and dignity. His begging was acceptable by society because of his condition. Nevertheless, if the blind man were to receive his sight, this would mean he now must own the responsibility to get a job and to work. Often, there are those who do not necessarily want their situation to improve or get better because it requires change and acceptance of new responsibilities. There are those who want money, but they do not want the responsibility of the job that comes along with earning money. Many are unable to stick with it until they get it because they are unwilling to accept the responsibilities of the things they are seeking. It is mandatory that if we want to stick with our goals until we achieve them, then we must be willing to accept the responsibilities that come with our ambitions.

The blind man stuck with it until he received his sight. By faith, let us continue to be encouraged in all that God has in store for us. Let us stick with the plans God has laid out for us until His will is done in them all. Let us take advantage of every opportunity that comes our way. Let us ask God to bless what we have; and let us use what we have to the glory of God. Let us trust God more and more to enable us to plow through discouragements. Moreover, let us be assured in our hearts of what we want and be persistent in pursuing it until we achieve it. Above all, let us remember that we can do all these things and so much more as we place our faith in God.

An anonymous author wrote the poem "Don't Quit". The poem says:

When things go wrong, as they sometimes will,
When the road you're trudging seems all up hill,
When the funds are low and the debts are high,
And you want to smile, but you have to sigh,
When care is pressing you down a bit,
Rest if you must; but don't you quit.

Life is queer with its twists and turns,
As everyone of us sometimes learns,
And many a failure turns about
When he might have won had he stuck it out;
Don't give up, though the pace seems slow;
You may succeed with another blow.

Often the goal is nearer than
It seems to a faint and faltering man,
Often the struggler has given up
When he might have captured the victor's cup.
And he learned too late, when the night came down,
How close he was to the golden crown.

Success is failure turned inside out;
The silver tint of the clouds of doubt;
And you never can tell how close you are,
It may be near when it seems afar;
So stick to the fight when you're hardest hit;
It's when things seem worst that you mustn't quit.

I trust the story of the blind man will encourage us to never give up. Let us not be quitters. Let us never throw in the towel until we reach our goal. Let us hang with it and hang in there until all is done. Let us be determined to be persistent in every good work and deed even against and amidst discouragements and setbacks. Let us not give up the fight for what is good; but let us strive to finish strong. Let us **stick with it until we get it**. If we are faithful in our pursuits, sooner or later, Christ will come to our rescue. He will open doors for us. Therefore, let us hold onto God's will for our lives. Let us build our hopes first on Him who is eternal, and then on those things which will carry us forward to victory. Amen!

10

FROM COMFORTABLE STRENGTH TO FRIGHTENED HELPLESSNESS BY A GREAT LOSS

This sermon encourages us to guard our reputations. No loss can be greater. There is no better personal treasure than our dignity and the respect of our character and virtue. To lose the goodness of our names is a significant and devastating loss that can damage us for a long time. In this sermon, Dr. Thomas provides guidance to help us maintain sound character and virtue.

Text: Judges 16:18-22 (KJV)

¹⁸ And when Delilah saw that he had told her all his heart, she sent and called for the lords of the Philistines, saying, Come up this once, for he hath shewed me all his heart. Then the lords of the Philistines came up unto her, and brought money in their hand.

¹⁹ And she made him sleep upon her knees; and she called for a man, and she caused him to shave off the seven locks of his head; and she began to afflict him, and his strength went from him.

²⁰ And she said, The Philistines be upon thee, Samson. And he awoke out of his sleep, and said, I will go out as at other times before, and shake myself. And he wist not that the LORD was departed from him.

²¹ But the Philistines took him, and put out his eyes, and brought him down to Gaza, and bound him with fetters of brass; and he did grind in the prison house.

²² Howbeit the hair of his head began to grow again after he was shaven.

On July 5, 2010, with the gentle touch of God's loving and gracious hand, I was awakened out of my sleep around 5:00 a.m. to finish packing and catch my 8:00 a.m. flight to attend the E.K. Bailey Conference in Dallas, Texas. Through the process of finishing my packing, making it to the airport, getting on the plane, and arriving in Dallas, Texas, I could not have asked for things to have gone or turned out any better for me. Everything that I had laid out the night before, I was easily able to pack into my suitcase. On the way to the airport, I thought about the long line that I would perhaps have to battle to get my ticket. Yet, I joyfully discovered upon arrival that I did not have to wait in line to obtain my ticket and check in my luggage. But I still had to go through the security check which is something I really dislike most about air travel. However, the time I spent going through security was like going through an empty self-check-out line in a grocery store. With the flight scheduled for about three hours, I set my mind on taking advantage of being in the air for three hours. Nevertheless, to my blessed surprise, we arrived in Dallas, Texas forty-five minutes before the scheduled time because of the flight pattern that was available for that time of the year. As the plane pulled into the gate where we were to exit, I was feeling really good that things had gone so well. But more than that, I was extremely excited about being at the E.K. Bailey Conference. I cannot begin to fully describe the good feeling I had as I was exiting the plane.

Unfortunately, the excitement and the good feeling did not last long. I began to check my pockets to reach for my wallet and I could not locate it. At that very moment, excitement began to disappear. The good feeling I had about everything suddenly went away. All the joys and expectations I had for the week quickly vanished when I could not locate my wallet.

I checked the bag that I carried with me on the plane and my wallet was not there. I was clearly on the verge of panicking and feeling helpless. There I was miles away from home in Dallas, Texas and I had nothing in my possession to identify me. I had no money or credit cards to purchase food, to process my hotel reservation, and to take care of other necessities. My demeanor instantly changed from being comfortable and relaxed to being frightened and helpless.

Without any previous thoughts on this matter, I became overtaken by how we can easily and quickly move from being comfortable in our strength to being frightened and helpless when we lose important things. There are things which are critical and essential to make our lives healthy and strong. But when we lose those things, we also lose so much more of ourselves.

A great example for us to consider is the life of a man named Samson. When Samson lost what served as the signature of his strength, he soon became frightened and helpless.

The story of Samson is fascinating. He was a man with supernatural strength. With his bare hands, he destroyed a lion. By himself, he also slew thirty men. With the jawbone of a donkey, he slew 1000 men. With his hands, he took hold of the city gates of Gaza (that is the doors, posts, lock, and all) and devastated the city. Truly, Samson was a man with indescribable and unusual strength.

If there is anything that can get us in trouble, it is taking things for granted. It is unwise to assume things will always be a certain way for us. It is sad to desperately need something, to think we have it, and to discover it is no longer there. Such is what happened to Samson.

Samson was in a predicament wherein he thought he still had his great strength. Samson loved a woman named Delilah who conspired against him on behalf of the Philistines. Through a series of events, Delilah convinced Samson to reveal to her the source of his strength. Upon learning the source of Samson's strength, Delilah lured Samson to sleep upon her lap.

While Samson was asleep upon her lap, Delilah had someone to come and cut off the seven locks of his hair. Samson woke out of his sleep thinking that he could fight as he had done before only to learn that the strength which he thought he had was gone. For he did not realize that while lying upon Delilah's lap, he had lost what he thought was the source of his strength. The Good News Bible says, *"Samson did not know the Lord had left him"*.

Samson was perhaps regarded as the Superman of his day. But now, after losing the source of his strength, he was put in prison in Gaza. He was bound with a bronze chain and made to work as a grinder in the mill with both of his eyes thrust out. What a great loss! Samson went from a man with comfortable strength to only become frightened and helpless.

The older I get, the more I wish I had known certain things when I was younger. I wish I had known in my teenage years and my initial adult years the value of certain virtues. I wish I had known how essential these things are to have a productive, strong, and viable character.

There are some virtues we must safeguard and protect. We must not lose our dignity, the goodness of our names, our integrity, or our self-worth. We cannot afford the loss of being trustworthy or truthful. The loss of these virtues can be catastrophic.

Thus, a relevant question to ask is, "How should we protect those critical virtues that help us remain comfortable and strong, and also help us avoid becoming frightened and helpless?" There are three points which the story of Samson encourages us to consider.

First, we must be careful with what and whom we come to love. Anyone who has ever had an experience with love knows that love is a good thing. But despite how good love is, it is not good to make a decision on the basis of love alone. I know that might sound strange, but please take note. Many people have been disappointed, hurt and destroyed by things that they came to love. Let us carefully observe the following as examples of love that have brought hurt or harm to many:

- crack, cocaine, other drugs,
- alcohol,
- the love for a woman,
- the love for a man,
- the love for gambling,
- the love for partying all night long,
- the love for shopping until the night of the day was done,

- the love for unhealthy food,
- or too much love for one's own selfish views.

Things such as these have turned out to be very damaging to many people's lives. Thus, we must know how to love some things and some people, but still know when the time has come to put those things or certain persons down and walk away.

That principle is nothing new to us. We understand this because, in many instances, we practice that principle perfectly. For instance, a woman sees a beautiful dress or pair of shoes she loves, but the dress or pair of shoes doesn't fit and she does not make the purchase. On the other hand, she may also take into consideration how buying those things might negatively impact other things she has to do. Consequently, she puts the dress or pair of shoes down and walks away.

Similarly consider a man who sees a nice suit or pair of shoes. He tries them on and dearly loves the suit or shoes, but the suit or the pair of shoes does not fit him. He also may consider how buying those things might negatively impact other things that have higher priority. As a result, the man puts the suit or pair of shoes down and walks away.

We all know from personal and practical experiences that having something we love which does not fit is going to be a problem. Before we see someone as one to love, it is good to first see if that person can fit as your friend.

Drs. Ella and Henry Mitchell in their book, *Together for Good – Lessons from Fifty-Five Years of Marriage*, tell how they were friends first and that their friendship grew into love and marriage. This is what Dr. Ella Mitchell shared about their relationship.

> *When Henry and I look back over a marriage that can stand ... we thank God that we did not start with a stereotypical passionate romance. Instead, we had three years in which to season and ripen a friendship based on our common value.... Friendship is far more important than we ever knew when we got married. Lasting love is not something people fall into. It is a combination of growing*

> *and climbing, and that happens through a profound amity*
> *that grows in the fertile soil of common values and interests.*
> *Together we have grown far beyond anything either of us*
> *had in mind fifty-five years ago, because God nourished our*
> *friendship and set it to blossom.*[48]

From the experience of Drs. Ella and Henry Mitchell, it is clear that if a friendship does not fit with the person we love, then that is not a person with whom we should unite.

Based upon where she was from, Delilah was not a good fit for Samson. Delilah was from the valley of Sorek which meant that she was a Philistine. It was not good for Samson, a Nazarite, to fall in love with a Philistine, the enemy of God's people.

Walking away from Delilah was not an easy task for Samson. A detail description of Delilah is not given, but her name meant long hair. From that, we can safely say that Delilah was an extremely attractive woman. So, we must give Samson a break for perhaps being drawn to Delilah. But despite how lovely Delilah might have been, Samson knew, as a Nazarite, that she was off limits for him.

We must understand that we are bound to lose certain virtues of our character when we move beyond our limitations, our principles, and beyond our values. For the sake of safeguarding these precious commodities, we must learn to walk from things and persons we may even love. Learning to flee from these things will keep us from losing those virtues which bring us comfort and strength, and which keep us from becoming frightened and helpless. Therefore, let us be careful with what and whom we come to love.

Second, we must not play games with our virtues. I do not know why anyone would want to play Russian Roulette. It is the game of putting a gun to your head with one out of six chances of being shot. Nevertheless, there are people who play this foolish game as a shout-out to the R&B song by the Spinners which says, *"the games people play."*

On the other hand, there should be some games we do not want to play. Furthermore, sometimes when we are playing a game, our opponent may have greater motivation than we do to win. We see this even in the story of Samson and Delilah.

When the Philistines learned about Samson and Delilah, the lords of the Philistine went to Delilah and offered her eleven hundred pieces of silver to find out the source of Samson's strength. The *Good News Bible* translation says five lords of the Philistines went to Delilah. This means Delilah was offered 5500 pieces of silver to get Samson to tell her the source of his strength.

From the scripture, we learn that Samson loved Delilah. However, we are not told how Delilah felt about Samson. Regardless of how she felt about Samson, it was not enough to stop her from trying to learn the source of his strength to gain the 5500 pieces of silver from the Philistines.

Instead of being frank when Delilah asked him about the source of his strength, Samson began to play games with Delilah. He told Delilah he would become weak if he were bound with seven fresh bowstrings that were never dried. Delilah tried this and found it was not true. After feeling mocked, Delilah asked Samson again to tell her the source of his strength. Thus, Samson told her that he would become weak if he was bound with new ropes that had never been used. Delilah tried this and found that it was not so.

Feeling mocked again while asserting that Samson had not spoken the truth to her, Delilah was persistent in her personal pursuit and again asked Samson to tell her the source of his strength. Samson continued to play games with Delilah. He told her that he would become helpless if she would weave the seven braids of his head into the fabric on the loom and tighten it with a pin (according to Judges 16:13, NIV). Again, Delilah discovered that Samson had tricked her.

Unfortunately, Samson played games with Delilah without knowing Delilah was being motivated to win 5500 pieces of silver for herself. She was persistent at this until she won. She tricked Samson into telling her all his heart, even the source of his strength. She made him sleep upon her knees and called for someone to shave his hair while he slept. Delilah afflicted Samson and his strength left him.

To prevent losing our virtues, it is imperative that we not play games with them. Let us be mindful that our opponents often believe their motives for winning are greater than our ambitions to safeguard our virtues. As they are persistent in trying to cause us to falter, let us be even more persisitent in safeguarding our virtues. Those who oppose us do not give up because they are losing. As they try harder to win, our persistence must be greater than theirs because the value of our virtues is far greater than anything.

Third, we must know when to shout, "wait a minute". Let me share an excerpt from an article about Nelson Mandela which appeared in Time Magazine on July 21, 2008 on page 44.

> *"In 1985 Nelson Mandela was operated on for an enlarged prostate. When he was returned to prison, he was separated from his colleagues and friends for the first time in 21 years. They protested. But as his longtime friend Ahmed Kathrada recalls, Nelson Mandela said to them, 'Wait a minute, chaps. Some good may come of this.'"*

Shouting *"wait a minute"* is a way to interrupt something we feel has gone on too long or something that has been questioned in a disrespectful way. Based on my experience, if we allow something to go on too long that is improper or allow something to be questioned disrespectfully without a challenge, it will be continued; and it will come back to haunt us.

After failing three times to learn the source of Samson's strength, Delilah went to Samson and said to him, *"How canst thou say, I love thee, when thine heart is not with me? Thou has mocked me these three times, and hast not told me wherein thy great strength lieth"* (Judges 16:15, KJV).

But the tragedy here is that Delilah went to Samson daily crying to him, *"How canst thou say, I love thee, when thine heart is not with me? Thou has mocked me these three times, and hast not told me wherein thy great strength lieth"*. Samson heard these words daily from Delilah.

Perhaps after the third day (giving Delilah a little break), Samson should have shouted to Delilah, *"Wait a minute, enough is enough"*. He should have stopped her. To protect his virtue, he should have ended her nagging rather than allowing himself to be put in a helpless situation.

Samson became weary over Delilah persistently urging him about the source of his strength until it vexed his soul unto death. Subsequently, he opened his heart and told Delilah the source of his strength. This would have never happened if Samson had just shouted *"wait a minute"*.

We need to know when to shout *"wait a minute"* to prevent us from losing the virtues of our character. This shout will comfort and strengthen us and keep us from slipping into fear and helplessness. The tragedy of not shouting *"wait a minute"* is that we may find ourselves sharing secrets of our heart with those who do not have our best interests in their hearts.

When I worked as a co-op student at Union Carbide in Oak Ridge, Tennessee, there were certain places inside the plant that were off-limits to me. The things in those places were extremely important to the safety and security of our nation. No one could walk into those places without proper authorizations. Similarly, we cannot share the secrets and the content of our hearts with people just because they are constantly nagging us. As we find these things happening, we must without hesitation learn to shout, *"wait a minute!"*

Certainly, it is time to shout *"wait a minute"* when someone is constantly nagging us about something we have not chosen or need to share with them.

Let us be careful not to lose our virtues. Such losses are subject to bring catastrophic changes in our lives.

As I prepare to close, let me share the entire story about my incident in Dallas, Texas as I was exiting the plane. After I discovered I did not have my wallet, I started crying out for help. I stayed near the exit door until all the passengers had gotten off the plane. Then I went to the flight attendants and told them my situation. I asked them to check where I was sitting. They went and looked, but they said that they could not find anything. I asked the flight attendants to look again and, upon going and looking again, one came back and shouted with joy, *"I found it."* All the joy and the enthusiasm that had vanished upon my arrival in Dallas, Texas immediately returned after I recovered my wallet.

Just in case we find ourselves in the process of losing our virtues, remember to cry out to God for help and God will restore. Samson cried out for help and God restored his strength.

In Joel 2:25-26 (KJV), God said: "²⁵ And I will restore to you the years that the locust hath eaten, the crankerworm, and the caterpillar, and the palmerworm, my great army which I sent among you. ²⁶ And ye shall eat in plenty, and be satisfied, and praise the name of the LORD your God, that hath dealt wondrously with you: and my people shall never be ashamed."

These words from the Prophet Joel are incredibly good words of hope when we discover our virtues are in jeopardy. Therefore, let us not be dismayed over our conditions nor over the predicaments we may face. No matter what betides us, let us take confidence in knowing God is a very present help in trouble. God will help us recover. He is able to reestablish our virtues if we only cry out to Him. Surely, He will take care of us. And He will restore us with the glorious virtues of His Beloved Son, Jesus Christ our Lord and Saviour. Amen!

11

THE DEMISE OF LETTING OUR GUARDS DOWN

We tend to put up our guards when we go into unsafe or unfamiliar places. This keeps us from being totally surprised and prepares us to react quickly if we suddenly face the unexpected. On the other hand, we are prone to let down our guards when we are in the company of people who appear friendly and trustworthy. We are not mindful that such situations may be positioning us to be used unmercifully. In this sermon, Dr. Thomas encourages us to be careful of letting down our guards when we are in what appears to be good company. Such negligence may result in a great demise.

Text: I Kings 13:11-25 (KJV)

[11] Now there dwelt an old prophet in Beth-el; and his sons came and told him all the works that the man of God had done that day in Beth-el: the words which he had spoken unto the king, them they told also to their father.

[12] And their father said unto them, What way went he? For his sons had seen what way the man of God went, which came from Judah.

[13] And he said unto his sons, Saddle me the ass. So they saddled him the ass; and he rode thereon, [14] And went after the man of God, and found him sitting under an oak: and he said unto him, *Art* thou the man of God that camest from Judah? And he said, I *am.*

[15] Then he said unto him, Come home with me, and eat bread.

[16] And he said, I may not return with thee, nor go in with thee: neither will I eat bread nor drink water with thee in this place: [17] For it was said to me by the word of the LORD, Thou shalt eat no bread nor drink water there, nor turn again to go by the way that thou camest.

[18] He said unto him, I *am* a prophet also as thou *art*; and an angel spake unto me by the word of the LORD, saying, Bring him back with thee into thine house, that he may eat bread and drink water. *But* he lied unto him.

[19] So he went back with him, and did eat bread in his house, and drank water.

[20] And it came to pass, as they sat at the table, that the word of the LORD came unto the prophet that brought him back: [21]And he cried unto the man of God that came from Judah, saying, Thus saith the LORD, Forasmuch as thou hast disobeyed the mouth of the LORD, and hast not kept the commandment which the LORD thy God commanded thee, [22] But camest back, and hast eaten bread and drunk water in the place, of the which *the LORD* did say to thee, Eat no bread, and drink no water: thy carcase shall not come unto the sepulchre of thy fathers.

[23] And it came to pass, after he had eaten bread, and after he had drunk, that he saddled for him the ass, to *wit*, for the prophet whom he had brought back.

[24] And when he was gone, a lion met him by the way, and slew him: and his carcase was cast in the way, and the ass stood by it, the lion also stood by the carcase.

[25] And, behold, men passed by, and saw the carcase in the way, and the lion standing by the carcase: and they came and told *it* in the city where the old prophet dwelt.

It is amazing, and sometimes it even seems unfair, how our lives can change so quickly. In one moment, we can feel like we are living on top of the world or walking on the clouds. Then within a moment, even faster than the blink of an eye, we can hit the bottom of the barrel with a great deal of pain and despair. Times such as these make life seem so unfair. Often it seems that things which take time, energy, and money to achieve should not be taken away by one mistake or one bad decision we may make later in life.

Unfortunately, I have known people who were living kind of semi-large, but something occurred that brought an immediate and unfortunate change to their lives. Such experiences as these teach us not to boast about where we are, what we are doing, or what we have. All can be lost or ruined ever so quickly. The old saying that we can be up today and down tomorrow is true. Yet we must also confess that we can be up today and we can be down before the day ends.

Since our status can change so quickly, it is necessary that we give attention to things which may cause us to fall when we have achieved certain heights in life. There are things that are beyond our control; but we should safeguard those things within our control.

The tsunami incident in parts of Africa and South Asia on December 26, 2004 was beyond the control of the people living in that region. Hurricane Katrina hit New Orleans in September 2005 and was a natural disaster beyond the control of the people of New Orleans. Likewise, Hurricane Sandy which devastated parts of New York and New Jersey on October 29, 2012 is another example of a natural disaster that was beyond the control of the people in its path in New York and New Jersey.

It is challenging for those on top of things to remain on top. If they are not careful and watchful, they may suddenly find themselves fighting to uphold their self-worth. Most likely they may come into that predicament in a moment when they let their guards down. In that moment, while their guards are down, something hits them; something overcomes them; something falls on them; something overpowers them; or something rushes upon them which they are not prepared to handle. Perhaps such incidents could be avoided or managed better if they would only keep their guards up.

The concept of keeping our guards up is nothing new. It is something all of us have been instructed to do in many areas of our lives. Consider the following as typical examples.

- For those who play sports, especially basketball, their coaches are constantly screaming to their players to keep their hands up to guard against their opponents.
- For those who serve or have served in the military, they are trained for warfare by their readiness to be on guard against unsuspected attacks.
- Mothers are forever warning their sons to keep their guards up against those foxy, fast moving young ladies who can crush and break their hearts.
- Fathers are constantly preaching, teaching, and screaming to their daughters to keep their guards up against wall street suit wearing entrepreneurs, billboard star athletes, and baggy-hanging and jive-talking young men who have only their selfish pleasures at heart.
- We all are reminded when traveling into certain cities, and especially when traveling abroad, to keep our guards up against various kinds of threats.

Before I was married, I dated a young lady working on her Ph.D. at North Carolina State University in Raleigh, North Carolina. She was from the Bronx of New York. She told me if I went to the Bronx of New York with her, we must constantly keep up our guards by looking across our shoulders to our left and to our right when walking to her house.

Keeping up our guards is a fundamental necessity. We all should understand how important it is for us to protect ourselves from mischievous acts. If we fail to keep up our guards, we are subject to be deceived and even destroyed.

We often have our guards up when we feel we are in danger;

when we are under surveillance or being watched; when we are in an uncomfortable place; or when we are around people we feel we cannot trust. Ironically, we are likely safest in the most dangerous predicament because we have elevated our guard against malicious or harmful acts.

On the contrary, the text for this message indicates that we have the tendency to let our guards down during times that do not appear to be dangerous. Unfortunately, such times occur when we are confronted with acts of kindness from those who seem to be kind. This is the case in our text of the prophet from Judah. Perhaps a quick review of the story would be beneficial.

The story in the text for this message begins by informing us that there was a prophet out of Judah whom God sent to a place called Bethel. As the prophet arrived in Bethel, King Jeroboam stood at the altar to offer a sacrifice unto God. As commanded by God, the prophet denounced the altar by telling Jeroboam that the altar was going to fall apart and the ashes on it were going to be scattered. When King Jeroboam heard that, he pointed at the prophet and ordered him to be arrested. As a result of this action, King Jeroboam's arm became paralyzed and he could not pull it back. Then the altar fell apart, and the ashes spilled to the ground as the prophet had said. King Jeroboam then asked the prophet to pray and ask God to heal him. The prophet prayed and God healed King Jeroboam. Out of gratitude, King Jeroboam invited the prophet to his house to eat and to receive a reward for what he had done. In response to King Jeroboam's offer, the prophet said to the King, quoting the Good News Translation (GNT): *"Even if you gave me half your wealth, I would not go with you or eat or drink anything with you. The Lord has commanded me not eat or drink a thing, and not to return home the same way I came." (I Kings 13:8-9, GNT)*

According to the scripture, the prophet did not go back the same way he had come but by another road.

The prophet's response to King Jeroboam's offer was right on. He had his act together. He was prophetic, powerful, and profound. However, we must be aware that regardless of how skillful, knowledgeable, and clever we are, there is always someone who is more advanced than we may be.

The text tells us that an old prophet heard what this prophet had done in Bethel. Therefore, the old prophet finds out the direction the prophet took to return home. And through a series of events, the old prophet finds the prophet from Judah and asks the prophet to come home with him. The prophet tells the old prophet, as he told King Jeroboam, that he could not go home with him because the LORD told him not to eat or drink anything and not to return home the same way he came.

Seemingly, the prophet from Judah still had it together. He acted as if he was in tune with what he was supposed to do. But things are not always as they appear. The old prophet convinced the prophet from Judah to go home with him. But sadly, as we learn in I Kings 13:23-24 (KJV), the prophet from Judah saddled up and rode off from the old prophet's house only to meet and to be killed by a lion.

The prophet from Judah was seemingly having a great day. He was figuratively like a person who was walking on water. Nevertheless, on the same day, his body is found lying on the ground.

How could this have happened? How did the prophet from Judah end up dead? Well, the simple answer is that he let down his guards when he began to accept an act of kindness from someone who appeared to be kind.

Yes, it is true that we are careful to keep our guards up when we feel we are in an unsafe or unsecure situation. But unfortunately, the prophet from Judah became defeated when he let his guards down over what appeared to be an act of kindness by someone who appeared to be kind.

So, the question we must ask is how do we keep our guards up when we are confronted with acts of kindness from those who appear to be kind? Let us address this question with three points.

First, we must never allow appearances to cause us to let down our guard. We are told from the text that it was an old prophet who invited the prophet from Judah to his house. An old prophet would perhaps be the least person we would feel the need to guard ourselves against. No one would think of an old prophet being harmful. We understand a young prophet maybe troubling for lack of experience, but we would not expect trouble from an old prophet. It is most likely that we would all feel comfortable in the presence of an old prophet because he would be like a father figure to us.

Nevertheless, we must remember Satan is a master of disguises. Satan will always come to us appearing as an angel of light or as someone who is nice and kind. He often appears as someone who embraces our values.

A person named B. R. White tells a story of the transport of illegal drugs in Harlem. The code word that was used for illegal drugs was "cake". To an outsider hearing that someone is bringing "cake" would mean someone is bringing something sweet and delicious to eat. But White soon learned that "cake" was the code word his father used as a drug dealer. It is instances such as this that we tend to let our guards down when it seems as though we are in good company that is promoting something good.

The saying is true that we cannot judge a book by its cover. Equally so, we cannot judge people's character by their appearance. Many men have been fooled by a beautiful looking young lady. Many women have also been led astray by a nice-looking young man. Thus, it is imperative that we not make decisions that are based solely on the appearance of persons or things. Something harmful could be underneath it all.

As a little boy growing up in a rural community, I would pick a nice-looking apple off one of the apple trees in my grandmother's backyard. After biting into it, I would become sorely disappointed when I found a worm inside.

By nature, a caterpillar emerges from its cocoon to become a beautiful butterfly with colorful wings. Yet underneath the wings lie the characteristics of a caterpillar.

We must not judge by appearance alone. Rather we must guard ourselves against actors and acts of kindness that come from unconfirmed sources.

Second, we must watch carefully those who claim they share our values. We naturally tend to feel comfortable around people with whom we feel we have something in common. Yet, we must know people will say and do things they feel are attractive to us when they are trying to win us over.

We tend to anchor ourselves with people who appear to have the same values we have. When the old prophet was trying to convince the prophet from Judah to come to his house, the old prophet said to the prophet from Judah, "I am a prophet as thou art." In other words, the old prophet was telling the prophet from Judah that they share the same values; enjoy the same things; think alike; and perhaps share the same outlook on life. Moreover, the old prophet was also telling the prophet from Judah that he could be trusted since he too was a prophet.

When President Obama traveled through southern Illinois after his first term in the Illinois legislature, he was reminded four times to only pack khaki pants and polo shirts. He was advised to pack no linen trousers or silk shirts. At the end of a week of travel, he recorded these words: *"I was sorry to leave. Not simply because I had made so many new friends, but because in the faces of all men and women I'd met I had recognized pieces of myself. In them I saw my grandfather's openness, my grandmother's matter-of-factness. The fried chicken, the potato salad, the grapes halves in Jello mold – all of it felt familiar."*[49] Thus he recognized he and the people of southern Illinois shared some of the same values after identifying with them.

Our values are not determined simply by what we say, but rather by what we do and how we do it. President Obama states, *"...one of the things that makes me a Democrat, I suppose-this idea that our communal values, our senses of mutual responsibility and social solidarity, should express themselves not just in the church or the mosque or the synagogue; not just on the blocks where we live, in the places where we work, or within our own families; but also through our government."*[50]

As we look back on the text, it says that the prophet lied. If the old prophet were truly a genuine prophet, he would not have lied to the prophet from Judah. Neither would he direct the prophet from Judah to disobey the LORD's command.

We must mark the person who tries to persuade or convince us to go against our values. Such a person does not truly share our values. We must therefore guard ourselves against such persons who tell us *"there isn't anything wrong with wrong; or what hurts will not hurt; or there is no reason to be afraid of trouble; or that everyone doing a thing is justification for us to do it too."* We must constantly guard ourselves against those who claim to share our values. In reality, they only want to persuade us to compromise our values for our demise.

Third, we must never allow others to make us question our guard. We do not need others to confirm what God has personally told us. We must be careful when people begin to question our guard.

We must also understand that some people have not been given a guard. No one ever told them what was right and what was wrong. Thus, they were never given a guard.

The prophet from Judah was given a guard. He was told specifically what to do and what not to do. The word of the LORD came to him personally. He was told by the LORD not to eat bread nor drink water in that place, nor turn home the way he came. Therefore, the prophet from Judah should not have allowed the old prophet to question what the LORD had instructed and directed him to do.

The old prophet said, *"an angel spake to me by the word of God."* Hearing that, the prophet from Judah should have immediately stopped the old prophet.

Here again, the old prophet said an angel told him, but the prophet from Judah said that the LORD told him. It was not appropriate for the prophet from Judah to believe the words of an angel over the words of the LORD which were spoken directly to him. It is like us believing what others say versus what our parents have said.

Let us be mindful that whenever someone tries to get us to question our guard, something important will always be left out. In the creation story, Satan said to Eve, *"Ye shall not surely die: For God doth know that in the day ye eat thereof, then your eyes shall be opened, and ye shall be as gods, knowing good and evil"* (Genesis 3:4-5, KJV). Satan was crafty and included something that appeared significant – *ye shall be as gods knowing good and evil* – while leaving or dismissing something extremely important. To Adam, God said, *"But of the tree of the knowledge of good and evil, thou shalt not eat of it: for in the day that thou eatest thereof thou shalt surely die"* (Genesis 2:17, KJV).

How many times has Satan deceived many with trickery, such as:

- Do not worry - you are not going to get pregnant.
- You are not going to get hooked on this.
- Just try it with me – it will not hurt you.
- We are not going to get caught.
- Let us have fun and rob this store – this will be the last time.
- You do not need to study to pass the test.
- Drop what you are doing and let us go party.

If we know our guards, then we must never let others force us to question them or to question their significance. If we know jumping from a building is going to cause us to fall then let no one force us to think differently. If we know fire will burn us, then let no one persuade us to think differently. If we know to steal, lie and cheat will cause us to pay a price, then do not let others tempt us to think differently. If we know that we must stay focused in school to have decent opportunities or else we will suffer great losses, then let no one, absolutely no one, convince us to behave differently.

We must keep up our guard. To have our guards down at the wrong time can destroy our lives.

It is certainly challenging and difficult for us to keep our guards up. Figuratively, our arms can only hold up but for only so long without rest. Our eyes can only stay opened but so long without some sleep. Our bodies can only function but so long without some food. Consequently, we need a place to go to let our guards down where we can find some solace, rest, and comfort.

The prophet of Judah was not forbidden to neither eat nor drink. He was forbidden to eat and drink in Bethel. Even so, we are never forbidden not to take our guards down. We just need to know the place that it can be done.

There is only one place where we can safely take our guards down. That place is in prayer with Jesus. An old hymn says: *Safe in the arms of Jesus, Safe on His gentle breast; There by His love, sweetly my soul shall rest; Jesus, my heart's desire refuge; Firm on the Rock of Ages; Ever my trust shall be.*

Another hymn says: *What a friend we have in Jesus; All our sins and griefs to bear; What a privilege to carry; Everything to God in prayer.*

We can be well assured that we can let our guards down before Jesus without fear. In Him we will find rest and peace. He is truly a comforting friend, a loving brother, and a faithful saviour.

The prophet from Judah should never have allowed the old prophet to question what God told him. Our best guard in life is to trust God and to take Him at His word. It does not matter how glamorous, how elegant, how kind, how colorful, and even how convincing others maybe, our guard is to take God at His word. Let us strive to live in obedience to God's word. By His word we will find wisdom and strength to guard ourselves against every evil attack.

12

BEWARE OF SATAN DISGUISED AS A FRIEND

Satan is effective at entrapping us through friendly disguises. So often he tries to destroy us by pretending to be a friend. In this sermon, Dr. Thomas instructs us to be mindful of Satan when he comes to tempt us through friendly disguises. The sermon is given to help us to discern and turn away from the reproach of the evil one.

Text: Luke 4:1-13 (KJV)

¹ And Jesus being full of the Holy Ghost returned from Jordan, and was led by the Spirit into the wilderness,

² Being forty days tempted of the devil. And in those days he did eat nothing: and when they were ended, he afterward hungered.

³ And the devil said unto him, If thou be the Son of God, command this stone that it be made bread.

⁴ And Jesus answered him, saying, It is written, THAT MAN SHALL NOT LIVE BY BREAD ALONE, BUT BY EVERY WORD OF GOD.

⁵ And the devil, taking him up into an high mountain, shewed unto him all the kingdoms of the world in a moment of time.

⁶ And the devil said unto him, All this power will I give thee, and the glory of them: for that is delivered unto me; and to whomsoever I will I give it.

⁷ If thou therefore wilt worship me, all shall be thine.

⁸ And Jesus answered and said unto him, Get thee behind me, Satan: for it is written, THOU SHALT WORSHIP THE LORD THY GOD, AND HIM ONLY SHALT THOU SERVE.

⁹ And he brought him to Jerusalem, and set him on a pinnacle of the temple, and said unto him, If thou be the Son of God, cast thyself down from hence:

¹⁰ For it is written, HE SHALL GIVE HIS ANGELS CHARGE OVER THEE, TO KEEP THEE:

¹¹ AND IN THEIR HANDS THEY SHALL BEAR THEE UP, LEST AT ANY TIME THOU DASH THY FOOT AGAINST A STONE.

¹² And Jesus answering said unto him, It is said, THOU SHALT NOT TEMPT THE LORD THY GOD.

¹³ And when the devil had ended all the temptation, he departed from him for a season.

Supporting Text: Genesis 3:1-7 (KJV)

There are times we encounter people wearing a disguise. You can almost be assured that whenever you encounter someone wearing a disguise that person is trying to prevent others from seeing them as they are. I have found that whenever people do not want to be seen as they really are, they are either trying to deceive or even destroy you.

Recall the story of **Little Red Riding Hood.** In this story, the wolf got into Little Red Riding Hood's grandmother's house by disguising his voice as the voice of Little Red Riding Hood. Then the wolf also was able to overtake Little Red Riding Hood by disguising himself as Little Red Riding Hood's grandmother.

People who have the desire to deceive and even destroy others with little resistance will use a disguise that is alluring to cover their evil intentions.

It is sad but people have used disguises since the creation of humankind. Even in the Bible people used disguises. For instance, Saul wore a disguise so that he could talk to a medium in Endor about Samuel. Tamar disguised herself as a prostitute to get the attention of her father-in-law, Judah. Then, there are false prophets in the Bible who disguised themselves as angels of light in sheep's clothing.

But would you believe that the first person in the Bible pictured as using a disguise was Satan? In Genesis, Satan appeared to Eve in the Garden of Eden in the form of a serpent. The way Genesis portrays Satan is not the traditional way Satan is presented to our children. Satan is often pictured as someone who is wearing black; carrying a pitchfork in his right hand; and having two big horns protruding from the top of his head with bulging eyes, a red face, a pointed mustache, and a mouth blasting fiery flames. However, I can guarantee you Satan will never approach us in such a traditional manner. Satan is not senseless. Satan knows that we are drawn to things that are attractive, lovely, kind, and pleasant; and not to things that are frightening. The scripture says, *"… for Satan himself is transformed into an angel of light."* (II Corinthians 11:14, KJV)

Now the way Satan approached Eve in the Garden of Eden proves that Satan is a master of disguises. Again, Satan came to Eve in the form of a serpent. Genesis 3:1 (KJV) tells us that *"the serpent was more subtil than any beast of the field which the Lord God had made."* In other words, the serpent was very cunning - smart, skillful, and crafty. Therefore, Satan approached Eve in a way that would not frighten her but rather would easily lure her.

A brother in the Lord shared with me once how his innocent little girl was deceived. She lost her whole check to a man who had disguised himself as a confused and lost foreigner. I repeat - Satan knows that we are drawn to attractive, lovely, kind, innocent, pleasant, and non-threatening persons, places and things.

Now the reason I want us to be aware of Satan's disguises is because of Satan's intent for our lives. Satan has only one ultimate purpose for our lives and that is to destroy it. Jesus said to Peter, *"...Satan hath desired to have you, that he may sift you as wheat."* (Luke 22:31, KJV) Then later Peter wrote in I Peter 5:8 (KJV), *"Be sober, be vigilant, because your adversary, the devil, like a roaring lion, walketh about, seeking whom he may devour."* Statistics, the media, and some of our personal experiences clearly show that the devil has sought out many of our young people; and the devil is sifting them like wheat. We are losing our African-American youth to drugs, alcohol, teenage pregnancy, laziness, low self-esteem, the bling-bling, and even satanic worship. We are now even losing them to suicide. African-American men make up 48% of the male prison population, and African-American women make up 51% of the female prison population. By the age of twenty, 41% of African-American women have given birth. In some of our urban cities, the dropout rates for African-Americans exceeds 50%. Only 55% of African-Americans over 16 years old are employed today. It is reported that nearly 100,000 African-American children carry guns to school. These statistics indicate how many of our African-American youth are being destroyed as never before.

Why are these things happening? I am quite sure there are many reasons. But among those, the one I want us to give attention to is our inability to recognize Satan's many different disguises.

I believe that one of Satan's most effective disguises being used against African-American children is that of a friend. I have to say that is a very clever disguise because a friend is normally someone with whom we share our dearest secrets. A friend is also someone with whom we let our guards down, and someone with whom we trust and share our weaknesses. We sing *"What a friend we have in Jesus"* because He is someone with whom we share our sorrows. He knows our weaknesses. Moreover, we have the privilege to commune with Him in prayer and find sweet consolation and peace for our souls.

Oh, how many innocent teenagers have been hurt by someone they thought was their friend? Not only teenagers, adults also have been hurt by people who were taken as their friends.

Alonzo Mourning points out in his book, *Resilience – Faith, Focus and Triumph,* that Len Bias thought those who gave him drugs (even cocaine) were his friends. You may recall that Len Bias was drafted with the second pick overall in the 1986 NBA Draft by the Boston Celtics, but overdosed on cocaine at a party at the age of twenty-two.[51] How unfortunate it is to discover the people we thought were our friends were just images of old Satan portraying himself as a friend.

It is so important that we not forget that a disguise is not the real thing. Therefore, anytime people pose as something they are not, they leave themselves unknowingly exposed because they are not being real. Therefore, if one is observant, one will know what to be on the lookout for and will be able to recognize Satan disguised as a friend.

After spending forty days and forty nights fasting and praying in the wilderness, the encounter Jesus had with Satan teaches us three things we ought to be aware of when Satan comes to us disguised as a friend. Before we look at these three things, it is important that we notice the time that Satan selected to tempt Jesus. Satan came to tempt Jesus after He had had a mountain-top experience. It occurred after Jesus had spent forty days and forty nights alone in the wilderness fasting and praying, getting closer to His Father. But when Jesus came out of the wilderness, the first person that Jesus met was Satan.

Young people, when things are going good for you, be careful — that could be the time Satan will try to disrupt your life. Great joy is often followed by great sorrow. Every high spiritual experience is often succeeded by seasons of peculiar temptations. When things are good for you, as you are pursuing your dreams and as you are on the verge of fulfilling your goals, please take heed and please be on the lookout for Satan who may be disguised as a friend.

According to our text, the first thing Satan does when he comes to us disguised as a friend is to target our physical vulnerability or our physical weaknesses. Do not play with Satan. Satan is very much aware of our physical weaknesses. He will not waste time approaching us with things that he knows are not a problem for us in the flesh. Satan targets us when and where we are vulnerably weak.

Jesus had fasted and prayed for forty days and nights. After being without food for that amount of time, Jesus was most definitely hungry. Therefore, without hesitation, Satan tempted Jesus at the very moment He was physically vulnerable. Satan said to Jesus, *"If thou be the Son of God, command that these stones be made bread."* (Matthew 4:3, KJV)

Now under the circumstances, the challenge Satan offered Jesus was very tempting. Jesus was hungry, and there was nothing wrong with Jesus satisfying his hunger. A person who has been fasting forty days and forty nights needs some food. However, the problem rested in the way Satan suggested to Jesus how He could satisfy His hunger. He told Jesus, *"command that these stones be made bread."* (Matthew 4:3, KJV) Satan was trying to get Jesus to satisfy His hunger without going through the process by which God had ordained. Satisfy your hunger without an acceptable and respectable job, and without the sweat on your face. The scripture says, *"In the sweat of thy face shalt thou eat bread"* (Genesis 3:19, KJV). Oh, dear young people, please take heed! The devil will always try to show us how we can have our hunger satisfied without going through the processes by which God has ordained. The devil says to us:

> *I know you want to wear designer clothes. I know you are hungering for this fancy car. I know you are hungering for this luxurious house. You can have all these things quickly by just selling drugs, using your body, killing, running games on people, and stealing. Do not worry about spending twelve long years in school, then another four to six years in college*

> *staying up studying late at night. Why do all that when you can command these stones to be made bread? Just name it and claim it.*

We must be careful of people who tempt us to take ill-advised ways to satisfy our craving and our desires by avoiding the process and the pattern God has ordained. Beware of such persons who may be angels of Satan disguising themselves as friends.

Secondly, when Satan comes to us disguised as a friend, he will show us how we might easily obtain the things of this world. The scripture says that Satan took Jesus up into an exceeding high mountain, and showed Jesus all the kingdoms of the world, and the glory of them within a moment of time (Matthew 4:8, KJV). Then Satan said to Jesus, *"All these things will I give thee, if thou wilt fall down and worship me"* (Matthew 4:9, KJV). Look at what Satan offered Jesus. Satan offered Jesus power and the glory that was associated with that power. However, the power that Satan offered Jesus was without responsibility. Satan never mentioned to Jesus the purpose of this power. Satan tried to appeal to the lowest element of human instinct which is power without responsibility.

Please do not misunderstand me, we need power. Nathan Wright Jr. says, "all men need power to become ... without power life cannot become what it must be." Jesus told his disciples to stay in Jerusalem until they were endued with power from on high. However, the power that was given to the disciples was for the purpose of helping them to carry out their responsibilities. Power was given to them so that they might be witnesses in Jerusalem, Judea, Samaria, and unto the uttermost part of the earth.

Charles Smith in his book, *The Church in the Life of the Black Family,* asserts "...to be created in the image and likeness of the Godhead is to be able to exercise responsible authority over things." In other words, God created man to be a responsible creature. Therefore, God gives man the power to help him carry out his responsibilities.

Going back to the text, let us take notice of how Satan tried to offer

Jesus power without responsibility. Sadly, power without responsibility appeals to our eyes. People want things without the responsibility that comes with those things. Watch out for people who want to give you power without responsibility.

Young people, please be careful. Please remember Satan is crafty. Satan did not offer Jesus power without a price. Satan said to Jesus, all this power I give to you if you would bow down and worship me. There is always a consequential price you must pay when you are willing to receive power without responsibility. To receive it, you must bow down. You will have to let go of your self-respect, your dignity, your good name, your self-worth, your values, your morals, and more importantly your God. Even if Satan gave you power without responsibility, *"What does it profit for a man to gain the whole world and lose his soul?"* Beware, oh please beware, of friends who come to you with a scheme that will offer you power without responsibility.

One of the distinct differences between Satan and Christ is their offering to us. Satan offers us the glory and the crown first and then destruction. Whereas, Christ offers us the cross first; but beneath the cross is the crown.

Lastly, when Satan comes to us disguised as a friend, Satan will try to make us prove ourselves with erroneous information. Satan challenged the identity and the relationship of Jesus as the Son of God by using the word IF. Notice Satan tried to put doubt in the mind of Jesus by challenging Jesus to prove himself by doing something silly based upon erroneous information.

It is Satan's job to put doubt in our minds, especially doubts about whose we are and what we believe. Satan told Eve, *"hath God said, Ye shall not eat of every tree of the garden?"* (Genesis 3:1) Then Satan said *"Ye shall not surely die."* (Genesis 3:4, KJV)

In your spare time, please look closely at our text, especially Luke 4:9-11 (KJV) which says: [9] *And he (Satan) brought him (Jesus) to Jerusalem, and set him on a pinnacle of the temple, and said unto him, If thou be the Son of God, cast thyself down from hence:* [10] *For it is written, HE SHALL*

GIVE HIS ANGELS CHARGE OVER THEE, TO KEEP THEE: [11] *AND IN THEIR HANDS THEY SHALL BEAR THEE UP, LEST AT ANY TIME THOU DASH THY FOOT AGAINST A STONE.*

Satan tried to persuade Jesus to prove Himself based on his definition of what it means to be the Son of God. But Satan quoted the scripture incorrectly. Satan quoted to Jesus Psalms 91:11-12 (KJV). However, Satan left out one important phrase in Psalm 91:11 (KJV) which says: *"For he shall give his angels charge over thee, to keep thee in all thy ways."*

Satan tried to get Jesus to prove himself based upon Satan's definition of the Son of God. But being the Son of God meant more than just turning stones into bread. Pharaoh's magicians were also able to turn their rods into a snake as Moses did. What I do does not necessarily make me who I am. Actors do it all the time. The characters they portray are not the persons they are.

The Son of God, according to the scripture, also meant one despised and rejected; a man of sorrow and acquainted with grief; one born of a virgin; one who would heal the sick, raise the dead, open the eyes of the blind, cause the lame to walk again, preach the gospel to the poor, heal the broken-hearted, and set at liberty them that are bruised; one who would suffer under Pontius Pilot and be crucified, dead and buried; and one who would be raised from the dead on the third day.

Emerson Fosdick has a book entitled, *The Hope of The World.* In it, Fosdick has a sermon entitled, **Six Ways To Tell Right From Wrong**. Fosdick says the first way to tell right from wrong is to submit it to the test of common sense. He says, suppose that someone should challenge you to a duel. What would you say? Fosdick answers by saying, *"I would advise you to say, do not be silly!"*[52]

On October 21, 1993, *The Raleigh News & Observer* printed an article about a sophomore at Shaw University who shot and killed himself while apparently playing a game of Russian Roulette in his dorm room? As you know Russian Roulette is a game in which one bullet is loaded into a revolver and players take turns putting the gun to their heads and pulling the trigger. Each pull advances the cylinder containing the bullet. Now I do not know what they were trying to prove, but the young man could have easily discovered Satan was disguising himself as a friend by simply using common sense to see that what he was doing was silly. What he was being asked to do failed the test of common sense. Beware of friends who try to make you prove yourself by doing things that do not equate with common sense. Without question, they are angels of Satan disguising themselves as friends.

Young people, Satan will come to you disguised as a friend. Satan's purpose is simply to sift you like wheat. But when Satan comes your way, you need to do as Jesus - speak the Word of God unto Satan. Tell Satan what is written in the Word of God. Tell Satan that man must not live by bread alone, but by every word that proceeds out of the mouth of God. Yes, say to Satan, *"get behind me Satan, I worship none other but the Lord God, and only him will I serve."*

I charge you that before you say anything to Satan, make sure that you have on the whole armor of God.

- Have your waist girded with the truth.
- Have your chest covered with the breastplate of righteousness.
- Have your feet covered with the preparation of the gospel of peace.
- Have the shield of faith within your heart.
- Cover your head with the helmet of salvation.
- Take the sword of the spirit which is the word of God.
- Pray always with prayer and supplication in the spirit.

And when you have done all that you can do, you just stand. Know for certain that God has not given us a spirit of fear, but of power, and of love, and of a sound mind.

13

MAKING THE MOST OF A RARE OPPORTUNITY

Each opportunity we have should be regarded as a special moment of life. Opportunities are not daily, regular, or routine occurrences. Some come only once in a lifetime; while others may repeat themselves when we least expect them. We must be careful to not let an opportunity escape us. We should do all we can to make the most of each of them. In this sermon, Dr. Thomas uses the life of Joseph to encourage us to make the most of every opportunity God gives us.

Text: Genesis 41:14-16, 39-41 (KJV)

¹⁴ Then Pharaoh sent and called Joseph, and they brought him hastily out of the dungeon: and he shaved *himself,* and changed his raiment, and came in unto Pharaoh.

¹⁵ And Pharaoh said unto Joseph, I have dreamed a dream, and *there is* none that can interpret it: and I have heard say of thee, *that* thou canst understand a dream to interpret it.

¹⁶ And Joseph answered Pharaoh, saying, *It is* not in me: God shall give Pharaoh an answer of peace.

³⁹ And Pharaoh said unto Joseph, Forasmuch as God hath showed thee all this, *there is* none so discreet and wise as thou *art:*

⁴⁰ Thou shalt be over my house, and according unto thy word shall all my people be ruled: only in the throne will I be greater than thou.

⁴¹ And Pharaoh said unto Joseph, See, I have set thee over all the land of Egypt.

There are times in life when we will be met by opportunities that can tremendously impact the brightness of our future. Those kinds of opportunities, I must say, do not come our way every single day like the rising of the sun. Usually, opportunities of this sort pass our way only once.

Admittedly, if we miss somethings today, perhaps we can obtain them the next time around. On the other hand, some opportunities are not repeatable. Often the opportunities that can make our future bright and healthy are the ones that do not tend to duplicate themselves. Certainly, they do not come our way every day.

Although some might see differently, life is a rare opportunity. In Psalm 102:11 (KJV), David says: "My days *are* like a shadow that declineth; and I am withered like grass."

The saying, *"There is always time,"* sounds encouraging; but it is not necessarily true as it relates to life. With life, we have only one opportunity to live it. If we fail to live life fully the first time around, we are not granted the privilege of a second time to live it again. Therefore, we should treasure every moment of life with the best we have to give.

I indeed cherish the words of an unknown author who wrote: *"I shall pass through this world but once. Therefore, any good, any kindness that I can show to any human being let me do it now. Let me not defer it nor neglect it for I shall never pass this way again."*

Since life cannot be repeated, we should cherish and honor each rare opportunity we have. For instance, I want our children to know that going to school is a rare opportunity. Besides our faith, I do not know of anything more tangible that will greatly impact the brightness of our future than an education. Oh, it might not seem this way, but what our children experience from Pre-K through twelfth grade is a rare opportunity.

Sad to say, but the privilege of getting an education has not always been readily available to African-Americans in this country. Even when the privilege was granted, the resources given to educate African-Americans were subpar and inadequate. I am grateful to those who taught me in elementary school, middle school, and high school.

However, the schools I attended were not as equipped, exposed, and enriching as schools fifteen, twenty, and thirty miles away from the community where I lived. Getting an education should be regarded as a rare opportunity. Therefore, it should not be mishandled.

Now let us consider a young man in the Bible named Joseph and observe how he responded to a rare opportunity. The stage from which Joseph teaches us is from a prison in Egypt. Through a series of events, Joseph was thrown in prison after being falsely accused of an attempted rape. After spending time in prison, Joseph, who was also a foreigner in the land of Egypt, became second in command in all of Egypt. Pharaoh set him over all the land of Egypt, even his household. Nothing could be done in Egypt without Joseph's permission. The Bible says in Genesis 41:42-43 (KJV):

> [42] And Pharaoh took off his ring from his hand, and put it upon Joseph's hand, and arrayed him in vesture of fine linen, and put a gold chain about his neck; [43] And he made him to ride in the second chariot which he had; and they cried before him. Bow the knee: and he made him ruler over all the land of Egypt.

Clearly, I can understand if you are raising questions such as:

- *How was Joseph, a prisoner, and a foreigner, able to go from the dark, damp, and dingy dungeon to riding in the chariot behind Pharaoh?*
- *How could a foreigner, who was a prisoner, become next in command to Pharaoh and be vested in fine linen?*

Thus, a young man, if you allow me to say, from the project, the hood, from the other side of the track, became next in command to Pharaoh. That was unimaginable and unthinkable. But it happened. Since it happened, what did Joseph do that propelled him from the dark, damp, and dingy dungeon to the second highest ranking position in the land of Egypt?

Let us closely review the story of Joseph. We note that Joseph's promotion from the dungeon to the second highest ranking position in the land of Egypt was the result of Joseph making the most of a rare opportunity. It was rare for a prisoner to be brought into the presence of Pharaoh. But this happened when Pharaoh had a dream that greatly disturbed him. None of the magicians and wise men of Egypt could interpret his dream. Pharaoh heard about Joseph's ability to interpret dreams. Pharaoh sent for Joseph. Joseph interpreted Pharaoh's dream, and the rest is history.

So, let us consider what happened to Joseph. Perhaps lessons learned from Joseph will help us to make the most of rare opportunities in our lives.

First, we make the most of a rare opportunity by being a dreamer. A man named Carl Sandburg said nothing happens unless there is first a dream. I have yet to meet a prominent individual whose life was not shaped by his or her dream. Carl Brasher, the first African-American deep-sea diver, and the first amputee to attain the rank of Master Chief Petty Officer and Master Diver, said that it was his dream that influenced him to become a deep-sea diver. What Carl Brasher accomplished was no accident because he was a dreamer.

Before accepting the call to preach the gospel, I worked with a prison ministry called Wake Fellowship. Wake Fellowship ministered to inmates in a prison known as Wake Advancement. I will never forget a conversation I had there with an inmate. During our conversation, I asked the young man what his plans were after getting out of prison. His response to me was, *"I do not have any plans. I have nothing to get out of prison for."* The young man was not thrilled with the possibility of getting out of prison because he had lost all his dreams and aspirations. Unfortunately, he was not even looking for an opportunity to get out of prison.

If you are not a dreamer, you will not look for opportunities. A rare opportunity will not appeal to you if you are not a dreamer.

Michael Vick "grew up in Newport News, Virginia in the Ridley Circle housing projects. This was considered to be a high crime area on the east end of Newport News. It was sometimes referred to as

'Newport-Nam' because it was like a jungle-like war zone with pitfalls and traps at every turn."[53]

Michael Vick's high school football coach was named Coach Reamon. He said to Michael Vick, *"You have to dream to get out of that neighborhood."*[54] Michael Vick dreamed about coming out of that neighborhood. He was able to get out of it by going to Virginia Tech University and then to the National Football League.

Joseph was a dreamer. He aspired for life. He sought for opportunities. His opportunity to interpret Pharaoh's dream came after he offered to interpret the dream of a butler who was a fellow inmate. Upon interpreting the butler's dream, Joseph said to the butler: *"But think on me when it shall be well with thee, and shew kindness, I pray thee, unto me, and make mention of me unto Pharaoh, and bring me out of this house."* (Genesis 40:14, KJV) Because he was a dreamer, Joseph sought opportunities to advance himself.

It is important that we dream. Our daily actions are influenced by our dreams.

Howard Thurman says that man becomes the living embodiment of what he dreams. In other words, what we hope to be tomorrow is what we should be working on today. Therefore, those who are dreaming of becoming a lawyer, doctor, engineer, preacher, teacher, scientist or whatever, should be working toward their dreams even now.

Having dreams will help our youth do well in school. Having dreams will enable them to see school as a rare opportunity for their dreams to come true.

Our dreams make us extremely careful of the things we do. To make the most of a rare opportunity, we must be dreamers. Langston Hughes was right when he wrote, *"Hold fast to dreams. For if dreams die, life is a broken-winged butterfly."*

Secondly, we make the most of rare opportunities by possessing self-love. Jesus taught to love our neighbors as we love ourselves. There is the tendency to place a lot of emphasis upon loving others, but hardly ever do we talk much about self-love. However, Jesus taught us to love others the way we love ourselves, which says we cannot love others until we first love ourselves. There is a big difference between being arrogant, boastful, and conceited versus loving ourselves, being proud, and having an appreciation for who we are. The Bible says that we were fearfully and wonderfully made.

Gary Collins wrote, *"self-love is not erotic or ecstatic self-adoration. Self-love means to see ourselves as worthwhile creatures valued and loved by God, gifted members of the body of Christ, bearers of the Divine nature."*

Self-love begins with a proper understanding of ourselves. We are special because we are valued and loved by God. We are gifted; we are blessed; and we are highly favored. Moreover, we are the bearers of the attributes of God. We are not God, but the image and likeness of God are bestowed upon us. Therefore, since God can create, even so we can be creative.

Now, self-love is manifested in good self-worth. Self-hate is a manifestation of low self-worth. Good self-worth is one of the most important possessions a person can have. When we have low self-worth, we can only do what others think we can do. How we feel about ourselves greatly impacts what we think we can do.

In Carl Brasher's book, *Men of Honor*, he shares the challenges he faced being an African-American trying to pursue his dream. Brasher wrote, *"Some people in the Navy may have used my race against me, but I never used race against myself. I have always viewed the color of my skin as a source of pride, strength, and inspiration."*[55]

Brasher did not allow the opinions of others to shape his view of himself. What is important is not what others think of us, but what we think of ourselves. A rare opportunity can be staring us in the face, but it is useless to us if we do not feel we can take advantage of it.

Do we avoid certain classes in school because we think we cannot handle them? What makes us think we cannot handle those classes? Who told us we were incapable of taking certain classes that are known to be extremely challenging? Who told us that we could not achieve certain heights? Are we allowing others to define who we are and what we can be? Or are we being who God says we are? God said we are fearfully and wonderfully made, and we are marvelous (Psalm 139:14, KJV).

Regardless of how his brothers ridicule him about his dreams, Joseph continued to dream because he possessed self-love. The Bible tells us God prospered all that Joseph did in the land of Egypt. I believe Joseph volunteered to interpret the butler's dream because he believed in himself. To take advantage of rare opportunities, we must possess self-love.

Lastly, to make the most of rare opportunities, it is imperative that we affirm ourselves. We must be careful that our sense of self-worth does not come from, or is not legitimatized, by others. When Joseph was called from the dungeon, the Bible says that Joseph shaved and changed his raiment. There is no indication that Joseph was instructed to do that. But Joseph simply affirmed himself. Joseph knew that he had self-worth. And he proved that he had self-worth be affirming himself.

Half the battle in upward mobility is how we present ourselves to affirm ourselves. Wearing clothes in such a way to bring negative attention to ourselves does not affirm our self-worth. We cannot take advantage of rare opportunities if we do not know how to affirm ourselves.

The San Diego Chargers had the first pick in the 2001 draft. Michael Vick thought that the Chargers would draft him as their number one pick. But to his surprise, the Chargers traded their No. 1 selection to the Atlanta Falcons. Later on, Michael Vick discovered that the Chargers became uncomfortable drafting him because of the friends Michael Vick brought with him to a workout. The Chargers believed that Michael Vick's friends would not be a positive influence in his life thereby making Michael Vick too great of a risk for them to take with the top pick. How Michael Vick's friends presented themselves caused the Chargers to lose faith in Michael Vick.

Dr. Booker T. Washington founded Tuskegee University in 1881. In his autobiography, he tells how he received admissions to Hampton Institute (now Hampton University). When Dr. Washington went to Hampton Institute, he did not have any money. For the class assignments, Dr. Washington had to report to the head teacher. To his regret, Dr. Washington's first appearance to the head teacher was not a favorable one. The head teacher, however, asked Dr. Washington, to sweep the recitation-room. In his autobiography, Dr. Washington wrote:

> *It occurred to me at once that this was my chance. Never did I receive an order with more delight. I knew that I could sweep, for Mrs. Ruffner had thoroughly taught me how to do that when I lived with her. I swept the recitation-room three times. Then I got a dusting-cloth and I dusted it four times. All the woodwork around the walls, every bench, table, and desk, I went over four times with my dusting-cloth. Besides, every piece of furniture had been moved, and every closet and corner in the room had been thoroughly cleaned. I had the feeling that in a large measure my future depended upon the impression I made upon the teacher in the cleaning of that room.[56]*

Dr. Washington said that after the head teacher had inspected the room, she said to him, *"I guess you will do to enter this institution."*[57] Although Dr. Washington had no money, yet he affirmed himself through his work ethics and his active attention to excellence.

When we are presented with rare opportunities, we must affirm ourselves. We must demonstrate that we are worthy of the opportunities given to us. If we want to attend Duke University, Harvard University, Yale University, Howard University, North Carolina Central University, Hampton University, Spelman College, Tuskegee University, Shaw University, Virginia Union University, Morehouse College, or any other prestigious college or university, then we must affirm ourselves. We must demonstrate that we are worthy of such opportunities as these.

My beautiful, gifted, young, sons and daughters, remember we are God's creations and the descendants of an honorable and glorious heritage. Therefore, let us use our inheritance to make the most of the rare opportunities given to us. Let us remember that we will excel in making the best of these opportunities by dreaming, by having self-love for ourselves, and by affirming ourselves.

I want to mention in closing something that Joseph said to Pharaoh that really struck me. Joseph said to Pharaoh, *"It is* not in me: God shall give Pharaoh an answer of peace."* (Genesis 41:16, KJV)

Hence, we must understand that rare opportunities are blessings from God. It was God who gave Joseph the ability to interpret Pharaoh's dream. God plays a significant role in the availability of rare opportunities. Carl Brashear says that when people ask him how he made it, he tells them that he made it by having faith in God, and by retaining a positive attitude and a can-do spirit.[58]

Having faith in God gives me the courage to take advantage of rare opportunities. And since it is God who gives us life, let us take advantage and make the most of every minute we live.

Dr. Benjamin E. Mays, past President of Morehouse College, famed these words: *"I've only just a minute, only sixty seconds in it. Forced upon me, can't refuse it. Didn't seek it, didn't choose it; but it is up to me to use it. I must suffer if I lose it, give an account if I abuse it. Just a tiny little minute, but eternity is in it."*

Only a minute but eternity is in it. A rare opportunity may be presented just for a minute, but eternity might be in it. To come to Jesus, it only takes a minute. It is a rare opportunity, but eternity is in it. We only have one opportunity to live this life, but through Jesus, there is a rare opportunity to have eternal life. It only takes a minute to come to Jesus. Yet, all of eternity is wrapped up in it.

14

Synchronizing Purpose and Time

Time is precious. We must have a special regard for it if we wish to live a productive and fruitful life. There are seasonal times we have to do certain things. To forfeit or disregard those seasons can result in a life without meaning or purpose. In this sermon, Dr. Thomas describes the important connection between purpose and time. He illustrates this truth by reminding us of the lessons we learn from dancing. Our movements must stay with the rhythm of the music; else, we will appear to be uncoordinated. Likewise, when we fail in our lives to synchronize purpose with time, then foolishness becomes our decorum, embarrassment covers our face, and regret becomes the song of our hearts. Consequently, Dr. Thomas strongly urges us to learn the importance of synchronizing purpose with time.

Text: Ecclesiastes 3:1 (KJV)

To every *thing there is* a season, and a time to every purpose under the heaven:

This sermon evolved out of a conversation I had with my nephew Preston who was 20 years old at the time the conversation occurred. On a certain day, Preston came to me and asked, *"Uncle Terry, where in the Bible does it say, 'to everything there is a season?'"* After asking the question, Preston went on to explain to me that a person by the name of Miklos Rozsa had a song entitled, *To Everything There Is a Season.* So, he wanted me to show him where the words to that song were in the Bible.

Without pondering, I knew the words to the song were taken from the Book of Ecclesiastes. However, I was not completely sure where those words were exactly located in the Book of Ecclesiastes. Therefore, I got my Bible and located the scripture in Ecclesiastes 3:1 for Preston.

Honestly, when I read Ecclesiastes 3:1 (KJV) on the day I shared it with Preston, it affected me in an immensely powerful new way. I had concretely internalized the phrase, *"to everything there is a season"* because my father would stroll through the house in the morning saying, *"get up, to everything there is a season."* But when I read the portion of Ecclesiastes 3:1 (KJV) that says, *"… and a time to every purpose under the heaven,"* it completely absorbed my mind's attention. For reasons that I cannot explain that phrase spoke to me on that day in ways it had not spoken to me before.

After much pondering, it eventually dawned on me that for a purpose to maximize its fullest intent, the purpose must be in sync with its time. In other words, I must know the right moment when the purpose of something should occur. Another way of saying that could be, I need wisdom to direct me to do the right thing at the right time.

The title for this sermon came while my nephew and I were taking a ride together. My nephew's father had passed. Since he and I were alone, I thought it was a good time for me to give him some sound advice in the form of an older man to a younger man type conversation.

As we were riding, things were reasonably quiet because Preston was listening intensely to a classical piece of music. I was shocked because on the nights before this day he was listening to what I describe as unexplainable loud rap music. As we were listening, he began to explain to me the difficulty of what the person on the violin was doing.

He tells me, *"the person on the violin is subdividing, and that is extremely difficult at the speed that this piece is being played."* And I said, *"uh huh."* I had no idea of what he was talking about. But then my moment came. I cleared my throat, and said:

> *Preston, the way you treat your girlfriend is really profound. You treat her with a lot of respect. Brother, don't ever lose that."*

After we discussed some personal matters about his relationship with his girlfriend, I said to him:

> *Preston, do you remember the passage of scripture you asked me to find in the Bible for you? Well, from that passage I have learned that it is not what you do alone that determines success but also the timing of the things that you do is equally important. Therefore, brother man, to get the best out of life, you need to make sure that you synchronize purpose with time.*

Thus, from this conversation with Preston, the Lord gave birth to this sermon.

I think one of the greatest challenges that young people in each generation face is the ability to synchronize purpose with time. My folks used to often say to me, *"Terry, you are moving too fast. It is not time now for you to do this, that, and the other. Do not rush it. When it is your time, you will be able to do it."*

I am going to confess something which 90% of all adults are probably guilty of. Many of the difficulties that we have encountered in life, more times than not, were a result of doing things at the wrong time. For instance, we did not intentionally get behind in our bills. But we got behind because we bought things, or we did things, at a time that we could not afford to do those things. Nothing was inherently wrong with what we bought or what we did. We just did it during a time in which it was neither an appropriate, beneficial, conducive, or necessary time for us. Subsequently, we created an unnecessary burden for ourselves.

I think each generation ought to want the next generation to profit from their mistakes. Most adults would say to our youth that it is extremely important to synchronize purpose with time. It is not only what we are doing, but it is when we do what we do that greatly impacts the outcome. For a farmer's crop to grow successfully not only must the farmer plant good seeds, but the farmer must also take into consideration the time in which the seeds are to be planted. Therefore, as we move in life, as we take our next step in life, as we face new encounters in life, we must scrutinize all that we do in relation to time. We must forever keep this question in the forefront of our minds, *"Is it time for us to do this?"* We do not want to find ourself doing things out of sync with its time. For example:

- We do not want to be hanging out of school when it is time to be in school.
- We do not want to be a parent when it is time to be a child.
- We do not want to destroy our minds when it is time to be developing wisdom.
- We do not want to give instructions when it is time to be taking instructions.
- We do not want to be talking when it is time to be listening.
- We do not want to be playing when it is time to be working.
- We do not want to be crying when it is the time to be laughing.
- We do not want to be in confinement when it is time to be free.

To do well in life, the purpose of the things we do must be done in sync with its time. As with dancing, our movement must stay with the rhythm of the beat. We look foolish when our steps are not in sync with the rhythm of the song. We must recognize that foolishness, embarrassment, and shame will result when we fail to synchronize purpose with time. Therefore, whatever we do, we must always synchronize its purpose with its time. For the remainder of this sermon let us examine three ways to help us synchronize purpose with time.

First, it takes discipline to synchronize purpose with time. The issue here is keeping purpose and time together. To keep purpose and time together, it takes self-control. One of the greatest virtues you can acquire as a youth is self-control. The Bible says in Proverbs 16:32 (KJV), *"He that is **slow to anger** is **better than the mighty; and he that ruleth his spirit than he that taketh a city."** Proverbs 25:28 (KJV) tells us, *"He that hath **no rule over his own spirit** is like **a city** that is **broken down, and without walls."**

In his essay entitled, <u>Man in the Mirror</u>, Gordon Parks wrote: *"No doubt it was wisdom that taught me that my most dangerous enemy could be myself."*

To have purpose in sync with time, we must have constraints and restraints. We cannot do things just because everyone else is doing it. We cannot do things just because no one else is watching. We cannot do things just because it appears to be the fun thing to do. We cannot do things just because we feel like doing it. It takes self-control for one to synchronize purpose with time. Certainly, we must recognize that self-control is a by-product of discipline.

Discipline writes Steven Barboza, *"...is home training and then some. It is the ability to round out your own rough edges, correct your own raggedy ways, curb your own appetite for things or people that are bound to get you into a world of trouble ..."*[59]

Jawanza Kunjufu gives an interesting definition for discipline in his book, <u>Developing Positive Self-Images & Discipline in Black Children</u>. He says, *"discipline is a set of rules and regulations exemplified by the leader (parent) that motivates followers (children) to model their behavior."*[60]

Craig M. Mullaney, a ranger soldier, often emphasized that he had to do more than just yell to cause his troops to take a particular action. In one of his books, he writes: *"I had to lead by example. If I wanted them to march faster, I had to march twice as fast with a smile on my face. If I wanted them to extend their threshold of pain, I had to push myself harder, and under no circumstances could I afford to whine. I woke up earlier; and then I went to sleep later than the squad every night. I said nothing, but they soon stopped complaining about fatigue."*[61]

So, for young people to develop the discipline that will help them to synchronize purpose with time, and to follow the rules and regulations they should adhere to, then it is important that parents and adults model such behaviors for them. *"Do as I say"* can only be influential when illustrated by the example of an adult or authority figure. Hence, for us to synchronize purpose with time, then discipline must be developed in our childhood.

Secondly, we must understand the importance of value to effectively synchronize purpose with time. On January 19, 1999, television host Larry King interviewed Madonna (the singer, dancer, actress, and director) during the Larry King Live Show. This interview had a great impact on me. Larry King asked Madonna would she ever get married. Madonna responded by saying, *"What's the point?"* In my estimation, Madonna's response was a question of value. She was trying to see the good or the value that was inherent in marriage.

To synchronize purpose with time, we must see the good or the value of doing certain things at a specific point in time. The biggest debate my family had with our youngest brother was why he should continue his college education when he was already making a few dollars. He would often say, *"what is the point of me going to school when I am making this amount of money?"* Clearly, he wanted to know the value.

We encourage our young ladies and men to wait until they are married before becoming sexually active. And their reply is, *"if I can prevent from becoming pregnant and prevent from catching a disease, what is the value in waiting, what is the good in waiting until I am married?"* Certainly, there is a lack of understanding the value of waiting and the value of engaging in such acts at the proper time and in the proper way.

People normally embrace things, an idea, or a principle when they can see the good that it will bring to their lives. In Matthew 13:45-46 (KJV), Jesus taught: *"45 Again, the kingdom of heaven is like unto a merchant man, seeking goodly pearls: 46 Who, when he had found one pearl of great price, went and sold all that he had, and bought it."*

We all must see the good and the value of synchronizing purpose with time. Someone said, *"Nothing can have value without being an object of utility."*

Therefore, when young people or others ask *"why"*, they want to know the good or the value behind responding to the guidance being given to them. Nevertheless, it is imperative that the question *"what's the point"* be answered so that we can display discipline in being able to synchronize purpose with time.

Thirdly, we must have governance to enable us to apply discipline and value in synchronizing purpose with time. I played basketball in high school. Whenever we played at another school, we always had to leave at a specific time. This was necessary to avoid rushing because the bus was governed. In other words, the bus was limited to a maximum speed of 60 mph. It did not matter how hard the bus driver pressed the gas pedal the bus would not go faster than 60 mph because it was governed by that speed. On the other hand, this governance was placed on the bus for our safety.

It does not matter how hard we try; it is just our human nature to attempt to do things out of sync with its time. Therefore, as with the bus, we need something to govern our lives to keep our purpose in sync with its time.

Actually to synchronize purpose with its time, we must aim to be in tune with God's plan for our lives. To have such governance upon us, we must seek first the kingdom of heaven and all its righteousness and everything else will be added unto us. Proverbs 3:6 tells us to acknowledge the LORD in all things — *"In all thy ways acknowledge him, and he shall direct thy paths."*

The governance we need to help us to synchronize purpose with time is the Spirit of God. The Spirit of God will lead and guide us into all truth. He will comfort us. But more importantly the Spirit of God, or the Holy Spirit, will keep us in sync with purpose and time.

Due to my own experiences, I want to encourage others to be wise by always synchronizing a purpose with its time. Therefore, I urge all of us to remember we must have discipline to synchronize a purpose with its time. Moreover, we must recognize the value of synchronizing a purpose with its time. And finally, it is critical that we yield to being governed by the Spirit of God.

Christians know and understand the importance of purpose being in sync with time because we look for Jesus to come back one day. We do not know the time of his return. He may come any day. He may show up anytime. He may come right now. But regardless of the time He comes, all things are certain to be well with us as long as we are ready.

The time when Jesus will return is known to none but God. Yet our responsibility is to be ready. If we are ready, regardless of the time the Lord Jesus Christ returns, we will have synchronized our readiness with His return. Therefore, let us be ready when He comes; and let us be found ready wheresoever we may be. Above all, let us be in sync with the time of Christ's return.

15

DEVELOPING MY INNATE BLESSING: LEARNING SELF-RELIANCE

Self-confidence is a vital character skill. It helps us to soar like an eagle. Self-confidence is the fruit of self-reliance. Self-reliance comes from developing the innate abilities God has given us. It is for such reasons that Dr. Thomas in this sermon expounds on the importance of learning self-reliance. He uses the analogy of a mother eagle teaching her eaglets how to fly to help us learn the virtue of self-reliance.

Text: Deuteronomy 32:11-12 (KJV)

[11] As an eagle stirreth up her nest, fluttereth over her young, spreadeth abroad her wings, taketh them, bearth them on her wings:

[12] So the LORD alone did lead him, and *there was* no strange god with him.

Without a doubt, the darkest moment in America's history was from 1619 to 1860, the period of institutional slavery. James Weldon Johnson says that period was so dark until it was darker than a hundred midnights. Unapologetically, I say that the darkest moment of any country's history is when it takes away the humanity and the human rights of another human being.

I often wonder how the institution of slavery with its perversion became part of the history of America. This seems so ironic given the nation's Declaration of Independence which states: *"that all men are created equal, that they are endowed by their Creator with certain unalienable Rights, that are among these are Life, Liberty, and the pursuit of Happiness."* How could sane human beings, living under the shadow of the Declaration of Independence, have the audacity to think that it was acceptable to enslave other human beings? It is shameful to think that it was acceptable to take people away from their homeland without their consent; place them in chains; package them like sardines in a can on a ship; strip them of their dignity; brand them; beat grown men and women mercilessly at will; work them unconsciously without pay; sexually abuse them; and then have the audacity to sing on Sunday morning, *"All creatures of our God and King."* How could another human being ever fathom or believe that such behavior was humanly and morally acceptable? But even more than that, how could that kind of behavior exist for more than two hundred years?

Although these things are beyond human comprehension, yet I know that for slavery to have existed as an institution, then it was also endorsed by society. Those who agreed to legalize it were brainwashed into doing so. But more than that, for slavery to have prevailed, something drastic also happened to those who were enslaved.

I do not quite understand it, but it is kind of difficult for me to comprehend why some of our ancestors had ambivalent feelings and mixed emotions about being freed from slavery. Booker T. Washington in his book Up from Slavery addressed this strange puzzling emotion. He asserts that when the Emancipation Proclamation was read to them in their slave quarters, there was great rejoicing, and thanksgiving, and wild ecstasy.[62] There was no feeling of bitterness towards their slave master. However, Dr. Washington also said, *"the wild rejoicing on the part of the emancipated colored people lasted but for a brief period, for I noticed that by the time they returned to their cabins there was a change in their feelings."*[63]

It is a matter worth pondering, "why was there a change in their feelings?" What was the problem? They were free! After two hundred plus years of degradation, why would a people have mixed feelings about their freedom?

Well, I am learning that the most effective weapon to use to retain a person in slavery is not the whip, but it is in the prevention of never allowing the person to learn self-reliance. Make a person a dependent human being and you will have a person who will be a slave for life.

Na'im Akbar in his book, Visions for Black Men, talks about what is involved in the transformation of becoming a man. Maleness, according to Akbar, is the initial stage in the transformation to mannishness. One moves from maleness to boyhood and from boyhood to a man. A person with a maleness mentality, says Akbar, looks to someone other than himself to take care of his needs. He has no initiative. He is totally dependent. Only when someone comes along and sticks a nipple in his mouth is he then capable of cleaning himself up. He is, in this mentality, declares Akbar, a whining, crying, hungry, and dependent little leech.

Akbar ascertains that the level of maleness is also the level of the slave. A slave is dependent; he is passive; he is totally waiting for his biological needs to be taken care of by someone else. And the people who developed and implemented the slave-making process understood that if they could keep the slaves locked into "maleness," a dependent stage, the slaves would stay dependent, non-rebellious, and they would not even respond. They would be passive when vital areas of their human existence were being violated. The reason why some of the slaves had mixed feelings when their freedom was announced was because their slave master never allowed them to ever learn self-reliance.

Regardless of how society supports the institution of slavery nothing keeps one in slavery like preventing one from developing the art of self-reliance. We learn from nature that to keep a bird on the ground, just prevent the bird from learning to fly.

Sometimes there is a thin line between helping someone and hurting someone. There are times that we do things for others in the name of helping them, but the help being given is hurting them. Any relationship where one person in the relationship depends on the other for assistance may get to the point where that dependence may become potentially damaging.

I understand that this really is a touchy subject in a parent and child relationship. Is there a point when help to our children can become a hindrance to them? I am of the opinion that the greatest harm that a parent can do to a child is to prevent the child from developing the art of self-reliance. When such happens, the child is being prevented from developing an innate blessing. To use the analogy of a bird, the child is being hindered from learning to fly.

In Joshua 17:15 (KJV), Joshua says to the tribe of Manasseh, *"If thou be a great people, then get thee up to the wood country, and cut down for thyself there in the land of the Per-iz-zites and of the giants, if mount E-phra-im be too narrow for thee"*.

The old saying is still true, *"Mama may have, father may have; but blessed is the child who has its own."* And for our children to have their own, we who are their guardians should give attention to things we may be doing that are hindering them from flying like eagles.

There are times when love must express itself in strange and tough ways. In my ethics class in seminary, we had to develop a definition for love. From the beginning, we concluded that love is just too deep to establish a definition. But for right now, I want to say that to love is to bring out the best in a person. Bringing out the best in a person sometimes comes in the form of pain.

In order to be politically correct, Matt Roloff would be considered a little person. But in addition to being a little person, Matt Roloff is also handicapped. He has severe problems in his legs, knees, hips, shoulders, arms, and the rest of his body. These problems make it impossible for him to stand or walk without the aid of crutches. Despite these things, Matt Roloff became a masterful, complex computer system designer.

Matt Roloff said his disabilities are part of everyday life and they are the things that made him who he is.

Speaking of disabilities, who would have ever thought that Israel's 40 years in the wilderness was God's way of bringing out the best in them? But it did! Their 40 years in the wilderness served as a means to prime the children of Israel to be ready to cross over the Jordan River to enter into the Promised Land. As a matter of fact, in Deuteronomy 32 (KJV), Moses explained to the children of Israel the reasons for their 40 years in the wilderness. God used those 40 years to teach the children of Israel self-reliance. To illustrate how God did it, Moses used the example of an eagle teaching her eaglets how to fly.

It goes without saying that an eagle is a fascinating bird. However, it is the eagle's flying ability that places the eagle in a class of birds all by itself. An eagle can fly 70 mph with ease. We see how big stalwart trees are brought down via a storm, but an eagle can fly through a storm. An eagle can fly up to the highest mountain. An eagle can even fly up in the clouds. Other birds fly together in a flock, but an eagle can fly alone. The eagle survives and sustains itself via its ability to fly quickly and swiftly. Before an eagle's prey can grab him or her, the eagle has flown quickly and swiftly away. An eagle's well-being, an eagle's strength, an eagle's safety, and an eagle's good fortune rest in its ability to fly. Disregarding the stubbornness of her eaglets, the mother eagle teaches them early on how to fly.

Slavery is not merely a matter of being in chains. It is also a matter of being locked outside of oneself and locked into other people. That is, one is always looking for others to do things he or she should be doing for himself or herself.

I regret this confession but when I was in high school, I passed many of my exams by utilizing the help from my cousin Hilton and my friend Jason. After high school, Hilton and Jason attended Alabama A&M University. I went to Tuskegee University. The tragedy of not having learned self-reliance emerged when I went to college. Things that I should have known as a freshman in college, I did not know. I really could not do well on some basic things. Consequently, I experienced many embarrassing moments. Unfortunately, I continued to encounter problems even after graduating from college and entering the Doctor of Ministry Program. From those experiences, I learned that you lose control of your destiny when you lock yourself outside of yourself. Moreover, I learned that when you fail to learn self-reliance, you also fail to learn how to fly.

As Christians, we need fellowship. We need intercessory prayer. We need wise counseling. Nevertheless, we are setting ourselves up for defeat when we are always relying on other Christians for guidance and for prayer. God has no respect of person. We all should have confidence in our personal relationship with God. We should be able to rely on our personal faith in God. If God saved us, God will also hear each of us.

We put ourselves in a bad predicament if we never learn self-reliance; or if we never learn how to fly; or if we never get a solid education. Learning self-reliance, learning how to fly, and getting a solid education are things we must do if we are going to be able to withstand the challenges of life. Therefore, I would like to share three things that the text suggests that are involved in learning self-reliance. Learning these things will equip us to fly like eagles and cause us to recognize and develop our God-given and innate skills.

First, self-reliance is a learned trait. It must be initiated and taught by someone who has learned self-reliance. If it had a choice, a young eagle would remain in its nest for its entire life. It would be satisfied sitting in its mother's nest, just eating the food that the mother eagle brings. On its own, a baby eagle never thinks about learning how to fly.

But our text in Deuteronomy reminds us that the mother eagle *"stirreth up her nest, fluttereth over her young."* Thus, the mother eagle begins the training of her young from the nest. The mother eagle knows how to fly. She also knows the importance of self-reliance. Therefore, she acts upon her awareness of the importance of these things and initiates the process of helping her young learn how to fly.

The way the mother eagle trains her young eaglets is quite fascinating. She tries to get them to leave the nest by flapping her wings over them, causing a lot of commotion. If that does not work, she brings rocks and sharp objects into the nest in order to agitate them and take away their comfort. And if that does not work, she destroys the nest, forcing the eaglets into a position where they must learn how to fly.

Professor Roland Jackson was one of my mathematics teachers in college. He holds a special place in my heart. I will never forget the day that I went to Professor Jackson to ask him to show me how to do a calculus problem. He looked at me and said, *"Do not ever come to me again to ask me to show you how to work a problem. You discover how to work it."*

I need to share with you something about Professor Jackson. He had po-li-o-my-le-tis, or you can say polio. He walked with a jerked limp. His body was curvaceous or curved. When he lectured, he always sat at his desk and wrote on an overhead projector because his condition would not allow him to stand for long periods of time. Yet, he was among the finest professors on the campus of Tuskegee University. Professor Jackson was very demanding of his students because he understood through his own experiences the importance of self-reliance. Therefore, he wanted us to learn self-reliance.

Others may see differently but I believe it is the responsibility of parents to initiate the process of self-reliance for their children. Remember, the mother eagle starts the training. She takes away the comfort. She destroys the nest. We must interact with our children in ways that enable them to learn to do for themselves.

During the preparation of this sermon, I was speaking to my sister (Annette Thomas) who lives in Birmingham, Alabama. In the conversation, she reminded me that our father always began his day early. He would rise early and awaken us to get out of bed to take care of our chores. In all aspects of his life and because of his personal trials being raised by his grandparents, he recognized (like the mother eagle) the importance of self-reliance and the importance of his children learning how to fly. And it is a fact, I sincerely believe he wanted to give his children (whom he loved) those character traits he found to be essentially important. For instance, he knew an education was important even though he was deprived of it. He understood the value of good work ethics. He recognized that rising early, being on time, helping others, and serving God were vital practices which he strived by example to instill in his young children.

Theologically, God looks only to himself. Therefore, God wants his children to learn self-reliance. When God said, *"let there be light"*, to whom was God talking? Job said God answers none but Himself. Moreover, God sometimes causes a commotion, agitation, and discomfort in our lives to get us to rely on His Spirit which He has given to us.

After forty years in the wilderness, the children of Israel learned that man does not live by bread alone, but by every word that proceeds out of the mouth of God. To learn self-reliance and to learn how to fly, someone who knows the importance of these things must initiate the process of helping us to learn them.

Second, to learn self-reliance, we must also learn to develop what we have been given. Have you ever noticed how commercials advertising various products always focus on how the products can make you better? Certain colognes make a man or woman irresistible. It is the type of sneakers that allow one to run fast or jump high. A beautiful young lady is speeding down the road in a sports car. She notices a guy. She stops and asks him, *"Are those Bugle Boys?"*

Commercials are designed to make people think that to be somebody or enhance yourself you need something outside of yourself. In my estimation, that creates many problems for young people. It causes them to think that they will be improved by things that are external or by things outside of themselves. However, the objective of self-reliance or learning how to fly is to develop that which has been given to us by our Creator. The mother eagle lets her eaglets learn to fly by getting them to use their wings.

God has already given us what we need to fly. Self-reliance is about developing what God has given us. When we were born, God gave each of us all we need to be outstanding. It is innate – it is within us. We must ask God to help us develop what He has given and put inside of us.

A person from whom I have gathered a tremendous amount of inspiration is Nick Vujicic who was born with no arms and no legs. Nevertheless, on his left foot, Nick Vujicic has two toes. With those two toes, Nick Vujicic plays music, dials his cell phone, and types. Nick Vujicic learned to use what he had. As a matter of fact, Nick Vujicic said that his life began to change when he stopped asking God for arms and legs and started using what he had.

Another person named Christy Brown was born with cerebral palsy. Subsequently, the only control that Christy Brown had over his body was his left foot. Nonetheless with that left foot, Christy Brown wrote over 1000 letters, wrote two bestsellers, and painted lovely pictures.

At birth, we all were to be intelligent. We were given a mind to reason, a heart to be compassionate, and a conscience to make sound decisions. But we must develop these precious God-given gifts.

Furthermore, we must be spiritually strong to do the right thing and rise above sin. God has given us the ability and the power to overcome evil. Jesus told his disciples that the Father would give them another Comforter, and the Comforter would abide with them forever. The Comforter would teach them all things. He would guide them into all truth. But more than those things, He would abide in them. Moreover, the disciples were not to leave Jerusalem until they were endued with power from on high. But we must learn to lean and be guided by the Spirit of God. Self-reliance is about developing our God-given gifts.

Finally, we must understand that we learn self-reliance and we learn how to fly under pressure. This might sound strange, but an eagle learns to use his or her wings by being forced to fly. When the baby eagle is forced out of the nest, it is suspended in the air. If the baby eagle does not use its wings, it falls quickly to the ground. It is through pressure, challenges, duress, fear, hardship, and even falling that the young eagle learns to fly.

Some of the greatest lessons which we and our children will learn will come when we are under pressure. We cannot take away every pain that our children bear. Equally so, God does not take away every pain that we bear.

Although I took swimming lesson in college, I never really learned to swim. But to get out of the class, we had to swim across a pool of water that was nine feet deep. Therefore, to pass the class, I jumped into the pool and started swimming. When I got half-way across the pool, I started drowning. The class instructor put a pole in the water for me to grab and pulled me to safety. Ironically, to teach me how to swim the instructor allowed me to experience drowning; but he did not let me drown.

When a baby eagle seemingly is not going to make it, the mother swoops under the baby eagle and catches the baby eagle on her wings. The baby eagle never hits the ground. The mother eagle allows her eaglets to experience falling; but she does not let them fall. Consistently, and perhaps unfavorably, we must allow our children to experience hurting; but we must prevent them from being hurt.

Peter experienced sinking, but God did not let him sink. Jesus experienced dying, but death had no victory over him. Paul said that we are persecuted, but not forsaken, cast down, but not destroyed (II Corinthians 4:9, KJV). God allows us to experience falling, but he does not allow us to fall. Self-reliance and learning how to fly are often best learned under pressure.

Young people, without question, we must learn self-reliance. In other words, we must learn how to develop our innate blessing. Moreover, it is also important that Christians learn how to fly.

Often, we sing with joyful energy this blessed hymn, *"I'll Fly Away"*. In the hymn, we share our hopes and dreams of looking for a glad morning. We do not know when it is going to be, but we know there is going to be a glad morning. We say we are going to fly to a home on God's celestial shores. We are going to fly like a bird from prison bars has flown. We are going to fly to a land where joy shall never end.

I must admit, I am a little puzzled how we will fly to a land where joy shall never end since we do not have wings. But on the other hand, I do not worry because the Word of God tells us that one day the children of God will fly away and be at rest. When we cannot rely on anything, we can rely on the Word of God which is the source of our self-reliance.

16

HELPING OUR CHILDREN TO WALK ON WATER

Life will present us with many challenges. Often, they will seem impossible or too overwhelming for us to overcome. Nevertheless, we must be willing to face even the challenges that appear to be too big for us. In this sermon, Dr. Thomas encourages us to face the challenges of life. He advises us to consider the rewards that await us. He describes the rewards as feeling that we are walking on water. Therefore, he urges us to accept and to conquer the challenges of life. Only then will we know and experience the joys of having walked on waters.

Text: Matthew 14:22-33 (KJV)

²² And straightway Jesus constrained his disciples to get into a ship, and to go before him unto the other side, while he sent the multitudes away.

²³ And when he had sent the multitudes away, he went up into a mountain apart to pray: and when the evening was come, he was there alone.

²⁴ But the ship was now in the midst of the sea, tossed with waves: for the wind was contrary.

²⁵ And in the fourth watch of the night Jesus went unto them, walking on the sea.

²⁶ And when the disciples saw him walking on the sea, they were troubled, saying, It is a spirit; and they cried out for fear.

²⁷ But straightway Jesus spake unto them, saying, Be of good cheer; it is I; be not afraid.

²⁸ And Peter answered him and said, Lord, if it be thou, bid me come unto thee on the water.

²⁹ And he said, Come. And when Peter was come down out of the ship, he walked on the water, to go to Jesus.

³⁰ But when he saw the wind boisterous, he was afraid; and beginning to sink, he cried, saying, Lord, save me.

³¹ And immediately Jesus stretched forth *his* hand, and caught him, and said unto him, O thou of little faith, wherefore didst thou doubt?

³² And when they were come into the ship, the wind ceased.

³³ Then they that were in the ship came and worshipped him, saying, Of a truth thou art the Son of God.

Years ago, I preached a sermon titled, *"Walking on the Waters of Life."* Of course, students of the Bible would likely guess that the sermon was based on Peter's experience in Matthew 14:22-33 (KJV) where he walked on water at the command of Jesus. The goal of that sermon was to encourage us to move beyond the limitations carved upon our minds by others. Then we will be able to enjoy the wonderful, beautiful, and thrilling things God has provided us.

Since that time, I read a book by Rev. Dr. J. Alfred Smith who is the former pastor of Allen Temple Baptist Church, Oakland, California, and a past President of the Progressive Baptist Convention. The book is titled <u>On the Jericho Road: A Memoir of Racial Justice, Social Action and Prophetic Ministry.</u> I consider the book to be a must-read for young pastors desiring a thought-provoking assessment or an evaluation of their ministry.

After reading Dr. Smith's book, the Spirit of God gave me to re-examine Peter's daring attempt to walk on water. The inspiration came after learning what happened to Dr. Smith at the end of his first year in elementary school. For a little background, Dr. Smith has authored or edited close to sixteen books. With such great accomplishment, it might be hard to believe that Dr. Smith's first-grade teacher recommended that he repeat the first grade because *"he could not master the printed word"*, as he phrased it.

In his book, Dr. Smith explained how his grandmother begged his teacher not to fail him. She promised his teacher that if she did not fail him, she would work with him during the summer months. Because of the persistence of his grandmother, his teacher accepted her proposal. Each day during that summer, Dr. Smith's grandmother would take him on the porch; sit him on her knees; open the huge family Bible; and, together with him, help him pronounce different words. Upon his return to school in the fall, his teacher could not believe what she heard. The following is his how Dr. Smith described it.

> *The teacher's jaw fell open. She jumped up from her seat and rushed out of the classroom .... Moments later, she returned with the principal in tow. 'Start reading again, child,' she*

commanded. *The principal stood behind the teacher with his hands folded in front of him. He raised his open palm in the direction of the open book. Once again, my reading was flawless* .... *She dropped a copy of Time magazine in front of me* .... *She snatched away the magazine and opened the geography book to a paragraph* .... *Again, I read. The teacher stared as though I had just walked on water.*[64]

Upon reading the last statement, my mind was overshadowed by the thought, *"helping our children to walk on water."* More importantly, I gained a new perspective of Peter's daring attempt to walk on water.

Now I admit, walking on water might seem dangerous, far-fetched, and ludicrous. Therefore, let me share my interpretation of it. I interpret walking on water as being able to master those things that were once elusive. It is to succeed in things that once were extremely difficult for us. It is being able to do things that appear to have been impossible or unlikely. As with Peter and with Dr. Smith, such mastery and success are the result of someone helping us.

Dr. Smith's story should encourage and inspire many students who might have failed or done poorly in the past. It should also be an awakening and a sense of hope for those concerned about the education of our children. It is amazing that within three months, Dr. Smith's grandmother helped him accomplish what nine months of training in public school could not do. Certainly, there are things we will not be able to do until someone who has a genuine concern for us takes the time to help us.

Our children can overcome their failures if there is someone who cares and is willing to labor with them as Dr. Smith's grandmother did for him. With such help, our children can learn to walk on water. Thus, the purpose of this sermon is to offer some guidance regarding three essential things that will enable us to help our children walk on water.

First, we must encourage our children to walk on water. Peter did not attempt to walk on water on his own intuition. Peter asked Jesus to bid him to walk on the water. Subsequently, Jesus told Peter to come.

Dr. Smith's grandmother encouraged him to practice reading every single day during the summer. I doubt very seriously if Peter and Dr. Smith would have walked on their waters without encouragement.

I have discovered encouragement is not just a matter of uttering hopeful and optimistic words. Rather, it involves being proof of those words. Jesus was walking on the water when he encouraged Peter to walk on the water. Jesus was influential and effective in encouraging Peter to walk on water because Jesus himself was walking on water. Dr. Smith's grandmother learned to read despite being denied many civil rights and liberties.

For our children to walk on water, they must have encouragement. This encouragement must come from those who are walking or who have walked on water. Those walking on water or who have walked on water are able to encourage and inspire others to develop the capacity to walk on water.

Socrates said, *"Let him that would move the world, move himself first."* Mahatma Gandhi once declared, *"We must be the change we wish to see in the world."*

Nick Vujicic, who was born with no arms and no legs, tells in his book, *Life Without Limits*, how a person by the name of Christy Brown was his hero. Christy Brown was a poet, painter, and author. However, because he was born with cerebral palsy, the only functional ligament Christy Brown had to do work with was his left foot. Nevertheless, with his left foot, Christy Brown wrote books and poems and made drawings. Subsequently, Christy Brown became an inspiration to Nick Vujicic who did work with the only functional ligament he had which were his two toes on his left foot. David Price, the owner of more than 350 golf courses, said to Nick Vujicic, *"… you have turned what should have been an incredible negative into something so positive."*[65]

The Late Rev. Ronnie Johnson was a dear minister friend of mine who needed a liver transplant. While needing the liver transplant, he told me he felt that he needed to show his people faith. Therefore, despite the severe pain and the personal discomforts of his sickness, he would preach from his pulpit. Sometimes he would even preach twice on Sunday's in his painful and uncomfortable condition. Seeing him preach on Sunday morning with so much pain, inspired one of his members to say to him: *"I know I have been hanging out and absence from the church. But if you can come to church and preach while swollen and hurting in your condition, then I promise you now that I will be at church every Sunday from now on."*

C. Vivian Stringer is the only women basketball coach to lead three different schools to the final four (Cheyney State, University of Iowa, and Rutgers University). Coach Stringer wrote the following excerpt in her book, Standing Tall:

> *In 1981, my fourteen-month-old daughter, Nina, lay in the hospital, fighting for her life. A missed diagnosis of spinal meningitis left her brain hopelessly damaged: my happy, dancing baby girl would never walk or talk again. In those early days, after being devastated, I looked to every quarter for comfort and counsel. A priest, passing me in the hospital chapel one night, suggested that perhaps this terrible thing had happened so that I could go on to inspire others, to give them hope.* [66]

Samuel Dewitt Proctor shared the following in his book, My Moral Odyssey:

> *...we learn from each other. As a boy I felt that something was reaching for my soul as I read the life of Helen Keller, the sightless genius, and the story of Booker T. Washington, with no money, walking from the Blue Ridge Mountains to the Chesapeake Bay to beg his way into college. When I read the lives of Fredrick Douglass, Madam Curie, and Harriet Tubman, the mental and emotional tides overflowed within me and the world became a different place."* [67]

Based on what Dr. Proctor shared, I conclude people who encourage us to walk on water must be people who can uniquely touch our soul. They enable us to see our predicaments in a different manner. In other words, it is what we see others do that uniquely affect our soul and cause us to believe that we can do what might appear to be beyond us.

Ronnie Raitt, an American blues singer-songwriter and slide guitar player, said of her mother, *"My mother was my dad's accompanist and music director, and I fell in love with piano through her incredible talent and love of playing. One of her greatest gifts to me was not making me take music lessons, just letting me come to it by her example."*[68]

Grammy winner Natalie Cole said her father, Nat King Cole, encouraged her by his example, rather than encouraging by his words. Our encouragement to others flows out of what we have gained ourselves. We encourage others to walk on water by our examples of persistence and being bold to use what God has given us. Through our personal experiences, we encourage others and prove to them that it is possible to walk on water.

Second, we must put those we are encouraging into the water. I do not want to be misunderstood. Therefore, I must share my definition of water. Water is symbolic of challenges that appear as too overwhelming or impossible for one to handle. If Peter could not handle the ship in the storm, then he surely could not walk on water during the storm. If Dr. Smith could not handle the first-grade reading, it would seem logical that the second-grade reading would be even more challenging for him. Nevertheless, Peter got out of the boat and stepped into the water. Equally so, Dr. Smith's grandmother took him from first-grade reading to second-grade reading.

To help our children walk on water, we must put them into the water. In other words, we must take them out of their safety zone. We must place them in situations that may appear to them to be overwhelming and impossible. Yet, we must reassure them that being in such challenging situations are not for a lifetime; but only for a moment to make them ready for a lifetime of being able to walk on water.

One of my mentors in ministry with whom I have great admiration is the Late Rev. Dr. Marcus Ingram. Dr. Ingram, who was blind, shared with me a story about a young man who came to college and failed the English Placement Exam. The young man was asked about his intended major and to this he replied that English was his intended major. Curious minds would have said to the young man, *"you are going to major in English, and you did not pass the English Placement Exam."* As the story goes, in four years the young man graduated with a major in English and with an excellent grade-point average.

We do not place our children in water because they know how to swim. We put them in water to learn to swim. Significant learning only occurs in situations that seem overwhelming and impossible.

The great inspirational author, Norman Vincent Peale, once said, *"Become a possibilitarian. No matter how dark your life seems to be, raise your sights and see the possibilities. Always see them, for they are always there."*[69]

To place our children in the water is to allow them to see new possibilities for their lives. In the words of Vincent Peale, it is helping them become *"possibilitarians"*.

Finally, to help our children walk on water, we must keep them focused. I had to learn that to accomplish certain things in life I must remain focused. We cannot be absorbed in an endeavor or activity if our minds are trying to give attention to many different things simultaneously.

Jackie Joyner-Kersee won the silver medal in the heptathlon event in the 1984 Olympic. She claimed that she did not win the gold in that event because she lost her strength and focus. The following is what she said:

> *I had dreamed about being in the Olympics, but you have to be mentally and physically ready to endure the ups and downs, the good and the bad, and figure out a way to be victorious. I thought that I was ready for that, but when you walk into the Los Angeles Coliseum with 100,000 people watching you and cheering for you-wow, [it] just hits you. And I was not ready. I ended up winning the silver medal that year, losing the gold to Glynis Nunn of Australia by just 5 points.... Five points out of 6,000 - that was all I needed. But I was not disappointed. It was the greatest experience I could have*

had as an athlete because it taught me an important lesson. I had a hamstring problem, but it was not as bad as I had made it out to be. But by thinking it was, each time I went to the starting line, I did not go thinking as a champion. I went to the starting line worrying about the pain, wondering where it was, wondering why it was hurting. Over two days of competition, I lost my strength and focus.[70]

It is hard for us to succeed when we lose focus. Peter was able to walk on the water as long as he kept his focus on the One he was relying, trusting and depending upon to enable him to walk on water. As he kept his eyes on Jesus, he was able to walk on water like Jesus. As he kept his focus on Jesus, he was encouraged by the example of Jesus and by his approval and endorsement.

Peter's words to Jesus were *"Lord, if it be thou, bid me come unto thee on the water"* (Matthew 14:28). In responding to Peter, Jesus simply said, *"Come"* (Matthew 28:29, KJV). Peter got out of the boat and proceeded toward Jesus walking on the water with no problem. But when Peter noticed the wind being boisterous, he became afraid and began to sink. Peter went from walking on water to sinking in water as he began to lose his focus.

I do not want to be hard on Peter. Under the same conditions, perhaps the average person would have done the same as Peter. Nevertheless, we are to learn from Peter's experience that we must maintain our focus. To help us maintain our focus, there must be something that keeps us grounded. We need something to believe and trust regardless of outside agitations and distractions.

Simply stated, to remain focused, we must have and keep our faith. Even though the wind was boisterous, it was important for Peter to continue to believe that if Jesus said come, he could still walk on water.

We must always remember that our focus is never on what we are doing nor on where you are, but rather where we are going. Peter's focus was not necessarily to walk on water. His focus was to come to Jesus and walking on water was a means to his destiny. To help our children walk on water, we must keep them focused on where they are going and not become distracted by the things around them. Remaining focused is not automatic; and it can be incredibly challenging. Therefore, it is important that we help to encourage our youth to remain focused on their destiny.

Newt Heisley was an airplane pilot in World War II. He spoke about an experience he had when he returned ten minutes late during cadet training. He shares his experience as follows:

> *"...one night some of us were given privileges to go to a nearby town for some rest and recreation. It was highly unusual for us to be allowed out at night. Unfortunately, I was ten minutes late coming back to base. The next day, I marched for ten hours to make up for my mistake. I was seldom late for something during the rest of my life."[71]*

Newt Heisley was given an experience to help him to remain focused ever after. Dr. Smith's grandmother kept him focused. Every day after the dishes were done and the chores completed, Dr. Smith's grandmother would take him out to the front porch and have him to read. The great actor Denzel Washington said that it was at the Boys Club in Mount Vernon, New York that he learned how to focus.[72] Michael Vick claimed that *"in connection with [his] grandmother's support, reading the Bible provided [him] a solid center and balance for [his] life. It kept [his] life focused."[73]*

Perhaps Peter had not grown sufficiently in his reliance, trust, and dependence upon Jesus. As such, he allowed the sound of the wind to remove his focus from Jesus. Therefore, we must also be careful where we place our focus.

Nick Vujicic confessed that when he went through his depression as a ten-year-old, he was relying on what he could see. His focus was on his limitations rather than on his possibilities.[74] That is why it is so important that we place our focus in something or in someone able to revive us regardless of what may come our way. A great lesson from which that can be learned is from Bethany Hamilton.

Bethany Hamilton aspired to be a professional surfer during her childhood. Her story of becoming a professional surfer is amazing when considering the obstacles, she had to overcome. While she was out surfing at age thirteen on a Halloween morning, her left arm was cut off almost to the armpit by a fifteen-foot tiger shark. Although she survived the incident, it would appear to most that her aspirations and dreams of becoming a professional surfer were over. It takes two hands to surf. Nevertheless, Bethany Hamilton stayed focused because she believed God had a plan for her; and no shark could take it away.[75] With one arm, she went on to become a professional surfer and in 2005 won the O'Neil Island Girl Junior Pro. What seemed impossible became possible because Bethany Hamilton's focus was based on what God had planned for her life.

To help our children walk on water, we must encourage them to seek to know and to remain focused on what God has planned for their lives. Jeremiah 29:11 (KJV) says, "For I know the thoughts that I think toward you, saith the LORD, thoughts of peace, and not of evil, to give you an expected end."

Without a doubt, I believe we can help our children to walk on the waters of life. If they begin to sink, Jesus will be there to prevent them from sinking. Remember Peter's desire was to come to Jesus. Remember, he said to Jesus: *"Lord, … bid me come unto thee on the water"* (Matthew 12:28, KJV). Therefore, in helping our children to walk on water, we must create within them a desire to come to Jesus and to do as He bids them to do. And if they do that, and trust Him, they will be able to walk gracefully and joyfully on the waters of life. Furthermore, if they find themselves sinking, all they need to do is to cry out to the Lord. He will reach out to them, lift them up, and keep them from sinking.

17

A Response to a Baby's Cry: Compassion

Strange and unusual behaviors may be signs that one is crying out for help. The behavior of many of our youth, especially many of our African-American boys, suggest they are crying out for help. In this sermon, Dr. Thomas emphasizes compassion as a proper response to those who are crying out for help. His sermon is taken from a well-known Bible story concerning Moses when he was an infant. The Bible says that Pharaoh's daughter showed compassion towards a weeping Hebrew baby boy who became Moses. Dr. Thomas uses this story to explain what it means to show compassion.

Text: Exodus 2:5-10 (KJV)

⁵ And the daughter of Pharaoh came down to wash *herself* at the river; and her maidens walked along by the river's side; and when she saw the ark among the flags, she sent her maid to fetch it.

⁶ And when she had opened it, she saw the child: and, behold, the baby wept. And she had compassion on him, and said, This *is one* of the Hebrews' children.

⁷ Then said his sister to Pharaoh's daughter, Shall I go and call to thee a nurse of the Hebrew women, and that she may nurse the child for thee?

⁸ And Pharaoh's daughter said to her, Go. And the maid went and called the child's mother.

⁹ And Pharaoh's daughter said unto her, Take this child away, and nurse it for me, and I will give *thee* thy wages. And the woman took the child, and nursed it.

¹⁰ And the child grew, and she brought him unto Pharaoh's daughter, and he became her son. And she called his name Moses: and she said, Because I drew him out of the water.

Before I make a statement on a psychological matter, I want to confess that I am not an authority on psychological matters. Whatever conclusions I may make concerning psychological matters are basically my opinions derived from my pastoral training, insights, and experiences.

Among all our human emotions, I contend that fear is one emotion that people are apt to give an inappropriate response. As Dr. Martin Luther King Jr., once said, *"we fail to understand that fear is a powerfully creative force."*

Greg Alan Williams holds that *"fear is a natural instinct we've all been given to help keep us safe."*[76]

Fear is normal, necessary, and healthy. Unfortunately, when we are confronted with fear, we tend to react incorrectly to it. This incorrect response may cause us to do some drastic things. A perfect example is how Pharaoh responded when the population of the children of Israel had grown significantly in the land of Egypt.

Fearing the growth in population of the children of Israel, Pharaoh began to genocide the male babies among the children of Israel. He first commanded the two Hebrew midwives (Shiph'-rah and Pu'-ah, see Exodus 1:15, KJV) to kill newborns that were boys. Because the midwives feared God they did not hearken to Pharaoh. Subsequently, Pharaoh commanded that every newborn Hebrew boy was to be thrown into the Nile River. Thus, Pharaoh is a clear example of how an inappropriate response to fear can cause one to do drastic things.

When one begins doing drastic things, then subsequently one will also most likely start doing unbelievable things to survive. For instance, to hide from the German during World War II, Charlene Schiff of Poland, at the age of 11, spent four days in the river with water to her neck. According to the April 2009 issue of Reader's Digest (page 149), Schiff *"spent two years in the woods alone. She slept during the day in a little grave she dug, and at night crawled out and searched for something-anything to eat"*. Another case in point occurred in 1994 when Immaculee Ilibagiza, a Tutsi of Rwanda, hid for 91days in a bathroom from the Hutus during their gruesome genocide against the Tutsi minority.

When faced with having to allude drastic and destructive dangers, one may embrace whatever means necessary in order to survive. Such was the case with the Hebrew family in our text from the tribe of Levi. As would be expected, this Hebrew family was trying to protect their newborn son from the wrath of Pharaoh's raging terror caused by his fear of the growing increase in the children of Israel.

After hiding their newborn for three months, it became apparent that other measures were needed to protect the infant from the wrath of Pharaoh. To save the child, the mother made a basket of tall jointed grass and covered it with tar to keep water from passing through it. After placing the infant in the basket, the mother took it and stationed it among the tall grass at the edge of the river. That was strange to me, but evidently the mother believed and trusted God to take care of her son. By the providential hands of God, the place where the mother put her child was in the area where Pharaoh's daughter came to wash herself. While she washed herself, she noticed the basket among the tall grass at the edge of the river and sent one of her maidens to retrieve it.

I have no idea what Pharaoh's daughter expected to see upon opening the basket. I would even think that there was some reluctance in opening the basket. But when she opened the basket, she saw the child. And the Bible says, *"and, behold, the babe wept"*. The presence of the word *behold* is here to inform us not to overlook the weeping child. Observe, tears were not just flowing from the baby's eyes, but the baby was <u>weeping</u>! In other words, the baby was crying with a loud voice of fear, anguish, distress, irritation, and vexation. I believe the Holy Spirit wants us to give special attention and intently observe the cry of this child.

The baby's cry was extremely significant. It touched the heart of the daughter of Pharaoh to the extent that she did not regard the child as a Hebrew. Moreover, she disregarded her father's decree that all newborn Hebrew boys were to be cast into the river. The baby wept in such a way that the emotions of sympathy and empathy arose in the heart of Pharaoh's daughter. For the text says, *"she had compassion on him"*. This means she showed pity towards the weeping child.

In my opinion, this story is significantly instructive and relevant for our times. We may not have recognized it yet, but we have many babies who are crying. Do you not hear them weeping bitterly aloud out of fear, anguish, distress, irritation, and vexation?

When I speak of babies, I am not necessarily talking about a child who is young in age. I am safe to take that position because *The American Heritage Dictionary* defines a baby *as a person who behaves in an infantile way*. One of the distinct qualities of infants is their inability to take care of themselves. The newborn Hebrew boy in our text could not take care of himself.

To further clarify my thoughts, let me share a script from Na'im Akbar's theory of transformation to mannishness found in his book, *Visions for Black Men*. Akbar says in the transformation to mannishness one moves from maleness to boyhood and from boyhood to a man. He says:

> *A person with a maleness mentality looks to someone other than himself to take care of his needs. He has no initiative. He is totally dependent. Only when someone comes along and sticks a nipple in his mouth is he capable of cleaning himself up. He is, in this mentality, a whining, crying, hungry, and dependent little leech.*

Literally, a baby is someone who at present cannot take care of themselves. Moreover, they cry as a way of expressing their need for help.

The behavior of many of our African-American boys is a matter worthy of prayerful consideration. For instance, many of them have fallen into one or more of the following traps:

- finding it difficult to function in school;
- leaving home for school but never making it to school;
- trafficking drugs;
- consuming an unbelievable amount of alcohol, cigarettes and drugs;
- exchanging a seat in a college classroom for a seat in a jail cell;
- becoming clueless about their future;

- joining gangs at an alarming rate;
- courting violence as a lifestyle;
- lacking a sense of self-esteem, self-worth and self-discipline; and
- escaping or fleeing safe havens, even their faith, the Church, and Christ.

Could it be this way because they are babies, and their behavior is their way of expressing their need for help? Yes, the Holy Spirit cries out to us from the text to *"BEHOLD"!* Let us **behold** this weeping generation. Let us prayerfully take note, contemplate, and pay attention to how our babies, our children, our sons, and our daughters are crying out for help.

On the other hand, the most relevant question to us is, *"What will be our response to their cries?"* Will we harshly say to them, *"shut-up?"* Will we just ignore it? Will we simply stick a pacifier in their mouths, and then continue on our merry way? Will we unassumingly place our hands over our ears so that we will never hear their cry? Will we quietly see them as a menace to society and put our fingers in our ears to drown out the sounds of their cries? Or, on the other hand, will we respond like Pharaoh's daughter? Remember, **SHE HAD COMPASSION**.

As the elect of God, our inner most being has been touched by the love of God. Therefore, we have the power within us to respond to the cries of our children with godly compassion. Such compassion makes us have a feeling of sympathy for those who have been victimized. It causes us to provide what is necessary and within our reach to rectify the victim's condition.

Perhaps we can more plainly see what it means to show godly compassion by observing the actions of Pharaoh's daughter. There are three principles illustrated by her that we wish to expound upon. May God use these three principles to help us develop the kind of compassion liken unto the kind He has shown us all. May He help us to respond aggressively as we hear the cries of our children. May He cause us to show godly compassion to the cries for help being heard from the young men and young women in our church family and in our community.

First, we are showing compassion as we realize the importance of noticing our children. When Pharaoh's daughter looked at the baby, she said, *"This is one of the Hebrews' children."* To make such a statement, it meant that Pharaoh's daughter had looked upon and given special attention to the child to recognize it as one of the Hebrews' children. She did not look at him and not see him. But by carefully noticing, examining, and observing him, she was able to see a distinction that set this child apart from among the Egyptians' children. Thus, she also recognized that this little baby boy was in trouble. For she said, as I repeat, *"This is one of the Hebrews' children."* It is extremely interesting and wonderful to observe how Pharaoh's daughter instantly began to show pity for someone whom her father commanded to be killed.

In the small rural town in Alabama where I grew up, it was almost impossible for one to skip school unnoticed. If you were out of school, and you were seen by an adult, the adult would always ask, *"Do your parents know you are not in school?"* And then the adult would say, *"I am going to call them and let them know I saw you today during the time you were supposed to be in school."*

Do we notice the number of African-American boys and girls walking the streets during the school hours of the day? Have we noticed how many of our children are not doing well in school? Have we noticed the things that our children are indulging in that are detrimental to them?

Without anyone saying a word to her, my mother could always tell when I had gotten in trouble at school. Why was this so? Well, it is because she noticed a change in my behavior.

When Nehemiah inquired of the condition of the city of Jerusalem, what he learned caused him to weep and mourn certain days, and to fast and pray before the God of heaven. During that time, King Artaxerxes noticed the change in Nehemiah's countenance without Nehemiah needing to tell King Artaxerxes that he was troubled.

We will never know the intricacies of a person's condition until we take time to notice them and to watch their behaviors.

We can constantly pass by something, and it will never affect us if we do not allow ourselves to notice it. The Bible describes Jesus as a man full of compassion. But whenever Jesus demonstrated an act of compassion it came as a result of Jesus noticing. The Bible says that Jesus **saw** the multitude and then Jesus healed them. Jesus **saw** the people as sheep without a shepherd and Jesus taught them.

Jesus also taught many parables (or stories) that were centered around compassion. He taught on compassion in the parable of the Good Samaritan. The Good Samaritan **saw** a man who had fallen among thieves, and *"he had compassion on him"* (Luke 10:33, KJV). In another story, Jesus taught on compassion using the parable of the lost or prodigal son in Luke 15. After the son had lost everything he had, he decides to return home to his father. As he was coming, and being *"a great way off, his father **saw him**, and had compassion, and ran, and fell on his neck, and kissed him* (Luke 15:20, KJV).

To respond with compassion to our babies' cries, we must first notice them. Using the words of Marvin Gaye, we show them that we are noticing them by telling them, *"C'mon talk to me, so you can see what's going on."*

Secondly, we are showing compassion when we give support. The role the sister played in the rescue of the Hebrew baby must not be overlooked. It is not uncommon; but sisters have always helped brothers get through.

When Pharaoh's daughter said, *"This is one of the Hebrews' children."*, the sister immediately said, *"Shall I go and call to thee a nurse of the Hebrew women, that she may nurse the child for thee?"* The sister's statement made Pharaoh's daughter responsible for the well-being of the child.

Again, take note of the sister's question to Pharaoh's daughter, *"Shall I go and call to thee a nurse of the Hebrew women, that she may nurse the child for thee?"* There is nothing openly stated, but perhaps the sister noticed the concern on the face of Pharaoh's daughter for the child. Seeing that concern motivated her to boldly ask that question.

Remember, the Hebrew baby boys were to be thrown in the Nile River, not nursed. Thus, the sister identified to Pharaoh's daughter what the child needed in order to survive. The child needed substance. The sister did not ask Pharaoh's daughter to personally give the substance. Rather, she asked her to provide the means whereby the necessary substance could be obtained. And Pharaoh's daughter's response was *"Go."*

Through Divine providence, the child's own mother was selected to nurse the child. But what is instructive here is what Pharaoh's daughter said to the mother of the child. Pharaoh's daughter said to her, *"take this child away, and nurse it for me, and I will give thee thy wages."* Pharaoh's daughter did not personally nurse the child, but she provided the support that was needed so that the child could be nursed. She provided the wages or the money for someone to nurse the child.

Many of the things our babies crying out for or trying to reach are figuratively beyond their reach. They are not tall enough, strong enough, perceptive enough, or wise enough to reach them. Many of the things causing them to weep are things they need but they are beyond their capabilities and capacities to obtain them. Simply, they cannot provide those things for themselves. Therefore, they need support. They need someone to care for their needs and to be concerned that their needs are provided. They need someone to encourage them along the way. They need someone to help them express themselves. They need someone to feed their minds, their hearts, their souls, and their spirits with wisdom and with wholesome and nutritious things that will give them a blessed life.

This should not be difficult for the children of God. For God gave us support to help us overcome sin. I will not leave you comfortless. But when the Comforter comes, or when your Support comes, He will come unto you and lead you and guide you and teach you all things.

If we are to adequately, and sufficiently, respond with compassion to our babies' cries for help, then it is necessary that we give them the support they need.

Finally, we are showing compassion when we take ownership. Observe that Pharaoh's daughter claimed the Hebrew child as her own. We must not overlook the ethnicity of the person who showed compassion on the Hebrew baby boy. To do so is to miss an especially important lesson.

Please remember, it was Pharaoh's daughter who showed compassion for the Hebrew baby boy. Yes, it was her father who issued a decree to kill all the newborn Hebrew boys. It was her father who saw the Hebrew boys as a threat to the nation of Egypt.

Pharaoh's daughter was not a Hebrew. She had no previous connection with the boy's parent. She had only known the best of the best. Certain trials and tribulations were not part of her society. She perhaps never experienced a poverty-stricken day in her life. Nevertheless, when the child grew, the Bible says that she claimed the child as her son. She claimed the child as her own and she gave the child the name *Moses.* It is just an observation, but perhaps it is not until we have assisted in pulling our children out of danger that we are truly able to give them a name.

What Pharaoh's daughter did for this Hebrew baby boy that was of another ethnic group is astounding. What makes it so astounding is that the Egyptians viewed the Hebrews as a menace to society. Hence, we do not have to be of the same ethnic group to show compassion to babies that are crying.

The September 2008 issue of Reader's Digest tells a story on page 148 about Charles Jenkins who was the Episcopal Bishop of New Orleans, and who was Eurocentric. During the recovery of Hurricane Katrina, Bishop Jenkins says that he told himself, *"My job is to make the comfortable aware of the powerless".* The powerless whom Bishop Jenkins was referring to were to the low-income residents of New Orleans who were predominately African-Americans.

We do not have to live in the same neighborhood to show compassion to babies that are crying. We do not have to be in the same economic standing to show compassion to babies that are crying. We do not have to share the same opinion as others to show compassion to babies that are crying. Gabrielle Douglas is an African-American who became the first US gymnast to take home a team gold Olympic medal and an individual gold Olympic medal. When she was 14 years old, she left her family in Virginia Beach to train with her coach, Liang Chow, in Des Moines, Iowa. While in training, she lived with Tavis and Missy Parton and their four daughters who were also Eurocentric.

I was overwhelmed to learn that Cindy McCain, the wife of Senator John McCain, adopted a baby girl from Mother Teresa's orphanage in Bangladesh. Clearly, those who have compassion do not regard the ethnicity of those needing or crying out for help.

We also learn from Pharaoh's daughter that to show compassion is to take personal possession and to feel the pain as if it were your own. Pharaoh's daughter saw the little Hebrew boy placed at the edge of the river and showed compassion by claiming the Hebrew baby boy as her son.

When I served as pastor of the Mount Zion Baptist Church in Madison, Wisconsin, a young guy named Raymond asked me a hard question. I was discussing an important matter with him, and he asked me: *"Why do you bother to care?"* Raymond's question caught me off guard. Well, in response to Raymond's question I said, *"I bother to care because I must see you and claim you as my own son."*

I thank God for the response of Pharaoh's daughter to the cry of the Hebrew baby boy. Because she showed compassion towards him, the child grew and became one of the greatest leaders and liberators the world has ever known.

Let us imagine what our crying babies could become if we showed them a little compassion!

Ben Carson grew up in the ghetto. But someone responded to his cry with compassion; and he became the first person to successfully separate Siamese twins from the brain.

Byron Pitts became an Emmy Award-winning journalist. This happened because a person by the name of Ulle Erika Lewes saw him in despair and had compassion on him. Lewes saw Pitts sitting on a bench crying on the campus of Ohio Wesleyan University. Lewes showed compassion towards Pitts and prevented him from dropping out of school.

Maya Angelou had a very humble beginning. Nevertheless, someone responded to her with compassion and she became a great African-American poet.

Oprah Winfrey came from a broken family and suffered an

abortion. Yet someone responded to her cry and she revolutionized television talk shows.

Stevie Wonder was born blind; but someone heard his cry when he was in grade school. Today, he is one of the greatest musicians the world has ever known.

As I close, let me share my love for the Lord Jesus Christ. Simply stated, I love the Lord with all my heart! He is so dear to me! I love Him because He first loved me. I love Him so very much because *He heard my cry and pitted my every groan.* He gave me the support to overcome sin. He paid the price for my sins to be remitted. Now He claims me and owns me as His child. And I will abide with Him, and He with me, forever and ever. Amen!

END NOTES

1   Don Gabor, *Big Things Happen When You Do The Little Things Right* (New York, NY: MJF Books, 1998), 101.

2   Matt Roloff with Tracy Sumner, *Against Tall Odds - Being A David in A Goliath World* (Sisters, Oregon, Multnomah Publishers, 1999), 87.

3   Meadowlark Lemon with Lee Stuart, *Trust Your Next Shot – A Guide to a Life of Joy* (Overland Park, Kansas: Ascend Books, 2010), 37.

4   Samuel DeWitt Proctor, *The Substance of Things Hoped For – A Memoir of African-American Faith* (New York: G. P. Putnam's Sons, 1995), 42.

5   Harry Emerson Fosdick, *Riverside Sermons* (New York: Harper & Brothers, 1958), 5.

6   Ben Carson, Gifted Hands (Grand Rapids, Michigan: Zondervan Publishing House, 1990), 27.

7   Ibid., 27.

8   Ibid., 10.

9   Dwight Gooden, Bob Klapisch, *Heat* (New York: William Morrow and Company, Inc., 1999), 147.

10 Michael Vick, *Michael Vick Finally Free an Autobiography* (Brentwood, Tennessee: Worthy Publishing, 2012), 163.

11 Howard Thurman, With Head and Heart (New York: A Harvest Brace & Company, 1979), 117.

12 Ibid.

13 Ibid.

14 Michael Vick, *Michael Vick – Finally Free An Autobiography* (Brentwood, Tn.: Worthy Publishing, 2012), 56.

15 Lauar Hillenbrand, *Unbroken* (New York: Random House, 2010), 182.

16 Ayaan Hirsi Ali, *Infidel* (New York: Free Press, 2007), 3.

17 Jawanza Kunjufu, *Developing Positive Self-Images & Discipline in Black Children* (Chicago: African-American Images, 1984), 15.

18 Samuel D. Proctor, *Samuel Proctor: My Moral Odyssey* (Forge Valley, Pa.: Judson Press,1989), 23.

19 Ronald W. Clark, *Einstein – The Life and Times* (New York: Avon Books, 1984), 27.

20 Ibid., 29.

21 Taylor Branch, *Parting The Waters: American In The King Years 1954-1963* (New York: Simon & Schuster Inc., 1988), 164.

22 Booker T. Washington, Up From Slavery (New York: Tribeca Books, 1965), 55.

23 David Von Lincoln, **Rise to Greatness – Abraham Lincoln and America's Most Perilous Year** (New York: Henry Holt and Company, 2012), 15.

24 .Nelson Mandela, *Long Way To Freedom - The Autobiography of Nelson Mandela* (New York: Little, Brown and Company, 1994), 393.

25 Ben Carson with Cecil Murphey, *Gifted Hands* (Grand Rapid, Michigan: Zondervan Books, 1990), 202.

26 Ibid., 201.

27 Nick Vujicic, *Life Without Limits* (New York: Doubleday, 2010), 55.

28 Denzel Washington with Daniel Paisner, *A Hand to Guide Me* (Des Moines, Iowa: Meredith Books, 2006), 126.

29 F. Washington Jarvis, *With Love and Prayers* (Boston, Massachusetts, David R. Godine, 2000), 15.

30 Mandela, 139.

31 ¹Harry Emerson Fosdick, *RiverSide Sermons* (New York: Harper & Brothers, 1958), 46.

32 Nick Vujicic, *Life Without Limits* (New York, NY.: Doubleday, 2010), 122.

33 Bethany Hamilton, *Soul Surfer* (New York, NY: Pocket Books, 2004), 180-181.

34 Vujicic, 195

35 Ibid.

36 Georgina Louise Hambleton, Christy Brown – The Life That Inspired My Left Foot (London: Mainstream Publishing, 2007), 94.

37 Tony Dungy, *UnCommon* (Carol Stream, Ill.:Tyndale HousePublisher, Inc., 2009), 39.

38 Ronald W. Clark, **Einstein: The Life and Time** (New York, NY: Avon Books, 1971), 27.

39 Byron Pitts, **Step Out on Nothing** (New York, NY: St. Martin' Press, 2009), 105-106.

40 Nick Vujicic, **Life Without Limits** (New York, NY: Doubleday, 2010), 132.

41 Alonzo Mourning with Dan Wetzel, **Resilience** (New York, NY: Ballantine Books, 2008), 105.

42 Nick Vujicic, **Life Without Limits** (New York, NY: DoubleDay, 2010, 12.

43 Daphne Gray with Gregg Lewis, **Yes, You Can, Heather!** (Grand Rapid, Michigan: Zondervan Publishing House, 1995, 19.

44 Byron Pitts, *Step Out On Nothing* (New York: St. Martin Press, 2009), 135

45 Ibid.

46 Ibid.

47 Ibid., 139

48 Ella and Henry Mitchell, **Together for Good – Lessons from Fifty-five Years of Marriage** (Kansas City, Missouri: Andrew McMeel Publishing, 1999), 15.

49 Barrack Obama, *The Audacity of Hope – Thoughts on Reclaiming the American Dream* (New York: Three Rivers Press, 2006), 63.

50 Ibid.

51 Alonzo Mourning with Dan Wetzel, *Resilience – Faith, Focus and Triumph* (New York, NY: Ballantine Books, 2008), 42.

52 Harry Emerson Fosdick, *The Hope of the World* (New York, NY: Harper & Brothers, 1933), 128

53 Ibid., 5.

54 Ibid., 17.

55 David Robbins, *Men of Honor* (New York: onyx Book, 2000), 6.

56 Booker T. Washington, page 56.

57 Ibid., 57.

58 Robbins, 5.

59 Steven Barboza, *The African-American Book of Value* (New York: Doubleday, 1998), 19.

60 Jawanza Kunjufu, *Developing Positive Self-Images & Discipline in Black Children* (Chicago, Illinois: African-American Images, 1984), 50.

61 Craig M. Mullaney

62 Booker T. Washington, *Up from Slavery*, 40.

63 Ibid., 40

64 Rev. Dr. James Alfred Smith, *On the Jericho Road* (Downers Grove, Illinois: InterVarsity Press, 2004), 31.

65 Nick Vujicic, *Life Without Limit* (New York, NY: Doubleday, 2010), 134.

66 C. Vivian Stringer with Laura Tucker, *Standing Tall, - A Memoir of Tragedy and Triumph* (New York, NY: Crown Publishers, 2008), 3.

67 Samuel Proctor, *My Moral Odyssey* (Valley Forge, PA: Judson, Press, 1989), 17.

68 Denzel Washington with Daniel Paisner, *A Hand to Guide Me* (Des Moines, Iowa: Meredith Books, 2006), 185.

69 Vujicic, 63.

70 Washington with Paisner, 126.

71 Steve Rabey, *Faith Under Fire* (Nashville:Thomas Nelson Publishers, 2002), 35.

72 Denzel and Daniel Paisner, 10.

73 Michael Vick with Brett Honeycutt and Stephen Copeland, *Michael Vick Finally Free an Autobiography* (Brentwood, TN: Worthy Publishing, 2012), 15.

74 Vujicic, 57.

75 Bethany Hamilton with Sheryl Berk and Rick Bundschuh, *Soul Surfer* (New York, NY: Pocket Books, 204), 2006.

76 GregAlan Williams, *Boys to Men* (New York: Doubleday, 1997), 48.

THE AUTHOR

Reverend Dr. Terry Thomas was born in Hurtsboro, Alabama on November 13, 1959. He was the fourth child of thirteen born to the Late Rev. Benjamin Franklin Thomas and Naomi Rowell Thomas. He was quietly taken by the angel of God into eternal rest on Saturday, April 23, 2016.

Rev. Dr. Thomas grew up in a rural community, where integrity, honesty, respect for elders as well as oneself, and the love for God were extremely important values. He constantly spoke of the training and guidance he received from his parents and the love he shared with his brothers and sisters. He considered his father as his primary role model and his mother as his silent force of inspiration. He counted growing up in Hurtsboro as a significant part of his adulthood development. He accepted Jesus Christ as his Savior during his childhood and became a member of St. Paul A.M.E. Church, Hurtsboro, AL.

Rev. Dr. Thomas earned his Bachelor of Science in Mathematics/Computer Science from Tuskegee University, Tuskegee, Alabama. After graduating from Tuskegee University, he was employed with IBM in Raleigh, NC as a Senior Associate Programmer for 15 years. During his employment there, he met Valerie Roberson. They married December 13, 1987. Upon moving to Raleigh, NC, he joined with Watts Chapel Missionary Baptist Church, Raleigh, NC. It was there that Rev. Dr. Thomas announced his calling to preach the Gospel of Christ. He preached his first sermon at Watts Chapel Missionary Baptist Church in 1986. Rev. Dr. Thomas passionately embraced the call to preach the Gospel of Christ. He committed himself to learning and studying the Word of God. Throughout his ministry, he devoted himself to reading numerous books. He had a special love for biographies and history to show others the many ways God works in the lives of people. Rev. Dr. Thomas also earned the following academic degrees: Master of Divinity from Shaw Divinity School, Shaw University, Raleigh, North

Carolina; and Doctor of Ministry from Samuel Dewitt Proctor School of Theology, Virginia Union University, Richmond, Virginia.

Rev. Dr. Thomas was a humble and faithful servant of Christ. He was a man of integrity who desired to imitate Christ in his earthly walk as a servant. He was passionate about the pastorate, about teaching and preaching the Word of God, and about caring for the flocks God had given him to shepherd. His pastorates included: First Baptist Church New Hill, New Hill, NC (1986 – 1997); Mt. Zion Baptist Church, Madison, WI (1997 – 2001); and West Durham Baptist Church, Durham, NC (2001 – 2015).

His gift and passion for teaching led Rev. Dr. Thomas to share his talents with several institutions of higher learning. He served as a doctoral mentor at United Theological Seminary in Dayton, Ohio. He also served as an instructor for the Pastor's Conference of the General Baptist State Convention of North Carolina. In addition, he was an instructor at Apex School of Theology, Apex, North Carolina, and at Union Bible College, Durham, North Carolina. Rev. Dr. Thomas was the former editor of the Baptist Informer, a publication produced by the General Baptist State Convention of North Carolina.

Rev Dr. Thomas was committed to Christian education and training. He impacted the lives of many ministers and laypersons as a profound seminarian, teacher, lecturer, and counselor. His heart was deeply rooted in helping others become "fruit-bearing disciples". He believed God's word provided divine inspirations to help them "make it through a storm". He wisely used God's Word to help others understand God's plan for "victorious living". Truly he dedicated himself to bring glory to God.

Printed in the United States
By Bookmasters